# Productivity Bargaining and Industrial Change

NORA STETTNER

Published for the Foundation on Automation and Employment Limited by

PERGAMON PRESS

OXFORD · LONDON · EDINBURGH · NEW YORK
TORONTO · SYDNEY · PARIS · BRAUNSCHWEIG

Pergamon Press Ltd., Headington Hill Hall, Oxford
4 & 5 Fitzroy Square, London W.1

Pergamon Press (Scotland) Ltd., 2 & 3 Teviot Place, Edinburgh 1

Pergamon Press Inc., Maxwell House, Fairview Park, Elmsford, New York 10523

Pergamon of Canada Ltd., 207 Queen's Quay West, Toronto 1

Pergamon Press (Aust.) Pty. Ltd., 19a Boundary Street, Rushcutters Bay, N.S.W. 2011, Australia

Pergamon Press S.A.R.L., 24 rue des Écoles, Paris 5e

Vieweg & Sohn GmbH, Burgplatz 1, Braunschweig

---



First edition 1969

Library of Congress Catalog Card No. 77-78064

---

*Printed in Great Britain by*
*The European Printing Company, London and Bletchley, Bucks.*



08 006756 5 (flexicover)
08 006757 3 (hard cover)

# Contents

*Contents*

# Foundation on Automation and Employment Limited
# Council of Management

# Foreword

At THE end of this valuable book Nora Stettner renews a plea for a much greater flow of information in industry so that management and workpeople can reach a better understanding of what is needed to raise efficiency and achieve a greater measure of social justice.

It is a plea which has my strongest support, especially at this point in our history when we in Britain are undergoing an often painful social, technological and industrial revolution.

We can never hope to cope with the bewildering pace of change in British industry—let alone fully exploit its potential benefit to the community—unless the men and women who have to make the changes in the office and on the shop floor really understand what is happening and why, and what is required of them.

Nora Stettner's study is an important contribution to that understanding because, so far as I know, it is the first general survey of the implications for industrial relations and the economy of that relatively new industrial phenomenon—the comprehensive productivity agreement.

Productivity bargaining, as a means of facilitating change, is one of the results of the period of reform we are now experiencing. But it is also of itself a tremendous catalyst for the reform of our industrial attitudes and the systems and institutions which regulate human relations in industry.

This book underlines the magnitude and the ramifications of the revolution on which we have embarked in recent years and the over-riding need for our managers, trade union officials and workers to keep on top of the process of change by continuously applying themselves to the problems of running a plant in an efficient and socially responsible way.

For a productivity agreement, as the author points out, is not a once and for all effort; it is a continuing exercise in managerial and trade union initiative and responsibility to ensure the efficient use of the undertaking's productive resources.

By putting productivity bargaining in perspective—and emphasising the need for effective planning at all levels if it is to be successful—Nora Stettner will help everyone to get their bearings in the dynamic world of industry. That is the main reason why I have great pleasure in commending this book to you.

Barbara Castle.

*"Under any Government in Britain, from the beginning of the Sixties onwards, we should have had to come to terms with the fact that we and every advanced industrial nation are going through a technological revolution whose pace and capacity for social devastation far outstrips any era of industrial and technological revolution in our history . . ."*

*"The task of a Labour Government is to direct change into channels which help to make the country strong. To stimulate change, but to control the pace and direction of change on a basis of national economic priorities. But equally, the task of a Labour Government is to temper change with a spirit of humanity and care for those who are affected by it."*

From a statement by the Prime Minister, HAROLD WILSON, at Newtown, Montgomery, 6 July 1968.

Chapter I

# What is Productivity Bargaining?

ALTHOUGH the concept of productivity bargaining is not completely new, it is only in recent years that it has become fashionable. Its popularity suggests that it meets a deeply-felt need. This is because it is well adapted to the requirements of industrial change. It has particular advantages to offer each of the major groups involved in industrial change—employers, workers and the government.

But there is reason to suspect that these apparent advantages look somewhat different to each of the three groups. The purpose of this book is to examine *what is expected from productivity bargaining by the various parties concerned*. From this perspective it should be possible to assess the significance of this well-publicised experiment.

This assessment requires an appraisal not only of whether the separate hopes of each group are justified, but also of whether they are consistent with each other. Only then can a sound guess be made as to whether or not productivity bargaining adds up to the revolutionary change in the British system of industrial relations which many commentators have pointed out has been made necessary by technological advance and economic change.

## What Productivity Bargaining Is

There have been many definitions of productivity bargaining, but they all stress the same basic feature. This is the acceptance of changes in work practices in return for improvements in wages, hours, working conditions or status.

This concept of an *exchange* is clearly emphasised in the following selection from the large number of definitions that have been put forward in recent years.

*The National Board for Prices and Incomes:* "Workers agree to make a change or a number of changes in work practice that will lead . . . to more economic working; and in return the employer agrees to a higher level of pay or other benefits."[1]

*The Royal Commission on Trade Unions and Employers' Associations:* "An agreement in which advantages of one kind or another, such as higher wages or increased leisure, are given to workers in return for agreement on their part to accept changes in working practices or in methods or in organisation of work which will lead to more efficient working . . . the concession on the workers' part must . . . be in specific concrete terms."[2]

*Allan Flanders:* "The concept of productivity bargaining . . . covers any type of collective bargaining in which an increase in the price of labour is associated with an increase in its productivity, regardless of how the latter is achieved. . . . The principle common to all productivity bargaining is the furnishing of an economic inducement for an acceptance of change . . ."[3]

*Alan Fox:* ". . . a method by which substantial wage increases and/or other improvements in the terms of employment are financed not through higher costs or prices, but by agreed changes in the work system which result in labour being used more effectively."[4]

*Jones and Golding:* "All these bargains offer some advances to the employees in exchange for specific changes in practices, in methods, or in the organisation of work which is intended to yield higher output and lower costs."[5]

*Engineering Employers' Federation:* "A productivity bargain can be regarded as a negotiation in which changes in wages are tied to changes in work with the object of reducing or stabilising unit labour costs; it is a constructive and comprehensive agreement

---

[1] National Board for Prices and Incomes, Report No. 36, *Productivity Agreements,* Cmnd. 3311, June 1967, p. 1.

[2] Royal Commission on Trade Unions and Employers' Associations, Research Paper 4, *Productivity Bargaining,* 1967, pp. 1–2.

[3] Allan Flanders, *The Fawley Productivity Agreements,* Faber, 1964.

[4] Alan Fox, "Productivity bargaining", *New Society,* 22 September 1966.

[5] Ken Jones and John Golding, *Productivity Bargaining,* Fabian Research Series 257, November 1966.

concluded between an employer and his employees so that there is a mutually agreed share of the ensuing benefits of cost reduction or stabilisation."[1]

But perhaps the simplest and most effective definition is that of Gunther Friederichs: "Productivity bargaining is bargaining to make change acceptable."[2]

The term "productivity bargaining" generally indicates a bundle of arrangements covering a whole range of measures for ensuring the most efficient use of labour in the plant as a whole. They include wage levels and structure, fringe benefits, hours, demarcations, work practices, manning agreements, shift arrangements, incentive payments, and so on—all as part of a package deal.

Productivity bargaining means just what it says—a negotiation process between workers and employers leading to a concrete contractual agreement to increase productivity. As with all contracts there must be, on each side, an incentive or "price" attractive enough to induce both workers and management to find better ways of doing the job.

For workers the inducement is usually more money; that is, higher pay. Sometimes, however, it is better hours with no reduction in earnings, greater job security, greater stability of pay, more generous "fringe benefits", enhanced job status (no more clocking in; longer dismissal notice; weekly, monthly or annual salaries and promotion rights) or increased participation in management decisions directly affecting workers.

The reverse of this coin is that management stands to gain equally with employees from the increased efficiency brought about through productivity bargains. There are many ways in which measures of the kind listed above will result in lower costs and bigger output. They imply more flexible use of labour, relaxation of demarcation rigidities, reduction of unnecessary overtime and of wasteful or redundant operations, a more efficient wage structure, fuller use of capital equipment, fewer unofficial strikes, more pro-

---

[1] *Productivity Bargaining and the Engineering Industry,* Federation Research Paper 1, March 1968, p. 7.

[2] Gunther Friederichs, in a personal interview, 1967.

ductivity-consciousness on the part of the workers and less resistance to technological change. Lower costs and bigger output make possible not only higher wages and better fringe benefits for workers, but also faster turnover and increased profits for employers.

## What Productivity Bargaining Is Not

A productivity bargain involves much more than exhortation to "productivity consciousness". Since it is a "bargain", it must go beyond pious hopes that workers will recognise the advantages to them of increasing their efficiency. It must offer them tangible inducements to do so.

Nor is a productivity bargain merely a change in production method—whether negotiated or unilaterally imposed. Such changes have been taking place as long as there have been employers.

> Surely one might say that the job of cutting down on expensive overtime, of introducing new machinery, of changing working methods to suit the new machinery, of attempting to do away with restrictions on output, of trying, in short, to find ways to stabilise or reduce unit costs, are things that conscientious and efficient business men are continually doing.[1]

To qualify as a productivity bargain, the change in method of production must be *mutually agreed with workers* in exchange for an improvement in their wages, hours, working conditions or status.

Productivity bargaining is also more than the introduction of or overhauling of, a system of payment which relates earnings to output. For decades, wage bargaining at the level of the workplace has taken output into account in the form of piecework, bonus payments or other types of incentive pay. But such bargaining has reflected the relative strength of the negotiating partners rather than the effect on plant efficiency.

There is an element of productivity bargaining in all schemes for payment by results (PBR), and many productivity bargains incorporate an element of PBR. But PBR is more limited in scope. It relates to a particular job at a particular time with a particular productive method; it has no effect on the overall organisation of

---

[1] Engineering Employers' Federation, *op. cit.*, p. 4.

work. PBR is designed to stimulate more *effort* on the part of a given worker. Productivity bargaining, on the other hand, aims at more effective use of resources. Hence it is broader than PBR and encompasses *changes* in methods of work, in work allocation, in labour practices and in flexibility of labour.

Finally, a productivity bargain is something different from a conventional collective bargaining agreement. Conventional agreements concern wages and working conditions but not the use of labour; in a productivity bargain, management identifies impediments to the efficient use of labour and negotiates with trade unions for their cooperation in removing these impediments. In a productivity bargain, pay increases are related to internal factors in the workshop; in a conventional wage agreement, increases are related to external conditions including cost of living and comparable wages elsewhere.

## Types of Productivity Agreements

Some productivity agreements are "partial"; others are "comprehensive"; and the majority range somewhere in between.

The purest type of partial productivity agreement relates to a single change in work practice and affects only a very limited group of workers. If it exchanges a concession to the workers in return for a revision of work practice designed to increase productivity, it qualifies as a productivity agreement. Usually the agreement is informal and undocumented. Such small-scale partial agreements have been common over the years as continuous work study has revealed the need for new methods of working in association with new methods of wage payment.

Comprehensive productivity agreements are relatively new on the industrial scene in Britain. They have much greater scope and depth than partial agreements. They cover a large number of related changes in work practice throughout the whole of the plant or industry. They embrace most of the workers engaged in production. And they are documented in detail in a formal written agreement.

Productivity agreements can also be differentiated according to the industrial level at which they are negotiated.

The unit embraced may be an entire industry on a national scale—as with recent agreements for the post office, the railways, electricity supply and the electrical contracting industry. Such agreements are comparatively rare.

It may cover a number of plants belonging to a single company—as with BOAC, BEA, Esso Wholesale Distribution, and British Oxygen.

It may be limited to an individual plant or workshop—as at Fawley and Milford Haven (Esso), Rogerstone (Alcan), Spencer (Richard Thomas and Baldwins), Coryton (Mobil Oil), and Shell Chemicals. This is the most frequent type of productivity agreement.

And finally productivity agreements may relate to a single department of a plant as the result of work study and revision of wage structure and methods of payment. Such partial productivity agreements are usually informal and hence undocumented, but they are widespread.

Productivity agreements normally cover manual workers in production, but they can also apply to white-collar workers in production or service industries. True, it is more difficult to measure output in services. But the essential requirement for a productivity agreement is to establish effective control of changes designed to improve utilisation of manpower. There is no doubt that this can be done with clerical staff as well as with manual workers.

An interesting example is the productivity agreement concluded between the Co-operative Insurance Society and the Guild of Insurance Officials. Under this agreement staff numbers are determined by the work load as measured in units of time. The time actually taken over work is recorded and compared with set targets. These controls allow for staff reductions which produce the main savings from the scheme. In return the staff received salary increases and a non-redundancy guarantee. Staff reductions are accomplished through natural wastage.

According to Robert McKersie,[1] the number of productivity agreements concluded in labour-intensive industries is about double those in capital-intensive industries. It has been assumed that pro-

[1] *The Significance of Productivity Bargaining*, paper presented at First World Congress, International Industrial Relations Association, Geneva, September 1967.

ductivity bargaining would only be feasible in capital-intensive industries where a large percentage of the labour savings could be shared without adversely affecting total costs. McKersie suggests that the explanation for this unexpected development is that productivity bargaining is more necessary in the labour-intensive industries due to the importance of labour costs and the competitive significance of potential savings from them.

McKersie also notes that most agreements are phased through time, but are implemented simultaneously across an organisation. "The phased approach is consistent with the notion that change should be executed gradually in order that one piece can be digested before the next is swallowed. However, the changes are implemented 'across the board' to avoid disparities and frictions within a company. ICI which has used the 'pilot' approach has experienced considerable internal tension between those who are 'experimenting' and those who are watching."[1]

## The Extent of Productivity Bargaining

It was the Esso agreement at Fawley, signed in July 1960, that started the current rash of productivity bargains in Britain. Since that time some 50 *major* agreements have been signed in Great Britain. These have probably not involved more than one million workers.

It is not possible, however, accurately to assess the number and coverage of productivity agreements currently in effect. Because many partial productivity agreements are informal and undocumented, there is no way of taking them into account.

Some indication of the number of agreements is available, however, from the Department of Employment and Productivity (formerly the Ministry of Labour) which receives applications for approval of productivity agreements under the prices and incomes policy. From January 1967 to July 1968 the Ministry of Labour examined about 1200 productivity agreements involving more than 800,000 workers. Of these, all but 95 were approved, many of them after modification in the course of discussions with the Department.

---

[1] *Ibid.*

About 200 productivity cases come to the Department every three months.

## Why are Productivity Agreements Negotiated?

Productivity agreements have to do with workshop issues which until recently were considered to be matters for unilateral management decision. Manpower utilisation and work practices at the plant level used to be determined by the employer and his staff of managers. Why are they now being subjected to *joint* decision by trade unions and employers through collective bargaining?

A full description of the many and varied motives which have led to productivity bargaining adds up to the contents of this book. At this point a brief summary sketch may serve as a useful preview.

1. *Productivity bargaining is a response to industrial change.*

There are many different kinds of pressures constantly at work which result in industrial change. Old industries like cotton, coal and railways are contracting as consumer demands alter. New industries are emerging to meet these demands—for example, synthetic fibres, oil, motor vehicles and aircraft. There is an accelerating process of industrial concentration as enterprises expand in size to reap the advantages of economies of scale in production—and of market power. As a result thousands of plants every year are involved in takeovers and mergers. As firms grow larger, management control shifts from owners—shareholders—to professional managerial staff. Above all, industry is changing as a consequence of technological developments.

All of these changes have an impact upon the way in which production is organised at the workshop level—and hence upon the development of productivity bargaining. They entail changes in job content; new kinds of skill; expensive and complicated machinery and equipment calling for more flexible use of manpower; the need for more efficient management with better control over labour costs; less job security; unstable earnings; and higher educational requirements for workers.

Thus the impact of change falls both on management and on workers and it is increasingly clear that neither can cope without the cooperation of the other. Because industrial change drastically affects the jobs, the security, and the incomes of workers, management can no longer introduce major changes without their assent. By the same token, because they recognise technological progress as the key to higher living standards and economic security, workers and their trade unions no longer resist change provided they can influence the way in which that change is introduced into their work lives. Hence the development of productivity bargaining.

2. *Productivity bargaining has also been stimulated by the overriding need for British industry to become more competitive.*

British firms are beginning to recognise that they must increase their efficiency and lower their costs to achieve a selling advantage on world markets. Many of them have become alarmed by their unfavourable ranking in cost comparisons, both at home and particularly abroad. OECD and EEC figures, for example, show that for a number of industries British output per man employed is far lower than in most other industrialised nations. (See Chapter IV.)

This lesson is also being driven home by government pressure from a number of directions—the National Plan, the little Neddies for industries, public exhortations and various inducements to increased efficiency. The government is motivated by its concern over the balance of payments situation. The economy has a long history of "stop-go". Periodic attempts to increase the growth rate have proved inflationary with demand outrunning production and leading to balance of payments crises and thence to deflation. All of these factors account for the present emphasis on productivity, particularly in export and import-saving industries.

3. *The development of productivity bargaining also reflects current labour shortages in Britain and the consequent need to use available manpower more efficiently.*

There is growing concern over shortages of manpower and of particular skills. Although the total population is expected to continue growing at 0.8 per cent a year, the work force will grow much more slowly. This is because of the declining birth rate, reduced immigration and more marriages at an earlier age.

4. Perhaps the greatest impetus to productivity bargaining has been the worries of employers, workers and the government about the persistent economic pattern in recent decades of alternating inflation and deflation, or "stop-go". Most individuals and economic groups are directly and adversely affected both by inflation and by deflation, but its most serious consequence relates to its effect on economic growth. Concern over economic growth, has in turn, given rise to the government's incomes policy. This is a complicated subject, and one that has an important bearing on productivity bargaining. Hence it will constitute the subject matter of the next chapter.

## Summary

Productivity bargaining is a process of arriving at agreement on changes in work practices designed to promote productive efficiency in exchange for concessions to workers concerning level and stability of pay, hours of work, working conditions and/or job security. Thus it is something different from mere exhortation, or isolated changes in productive methods, or changes in methods of payment, or conventional collective bargaining on wages and working conditions.

A productivity agreement may relate to a single change in practice affecting only a limited number of workers, or it may cover major changes embracing most of the workers throughout the production unit. Most productivity agreements are somewhere in between. Productivity agreements may cover an entire industry, a multi-plant enterprise, a single plant, or only one department of a plant. There are no reliable estimates of the current coverage of productivity agreements, but the number of workers involved is probably far less than two millions.

Productivity bargaining has been largely a response to industrial change and to labour shortages which make it essential to use manpower more effectively. Employers need the cooperation of workers in coping with such change, but this will be forthcoming only if workers can be assured of protection against the adverse effects of change. Without such cooperation there is little hope of making British exports more competitive in foreign markets and thus of solving the problem of sustained *economic growth.*

Chapter II

# Productivity Bargaining and Economic Growth

## Inflation and Economic Growth

*Cost-Push Inflation*

Why do prices keep on rising over the years?

The classical economists put their trust in the automatic functioning of the free market. They pictured an economy made up of hundreds of thousands of individual workers and producers, sellers and buyers not one of whom had any independent influence over this autonomous "market". No individual manufacturer or trader or customer controlled a large enough share of the total to be able to decide the price at which a product would sell. Similarly, no worker could decide the price (wage) at which he could sell his services. All prices were determined in the market by the total demand for and the total supply of the particular product or service.

In this textbook model of a market, prices fall as the economy becomes more industrialised. Technological progress implies more efficient methods of production. Costs per unit are constantly reduced as more money is invested in more and better productive equipment. Hence the general price level ought to decline year after year allowing consumers to reap the fruits of technological progress.

Yet the problem we are wrestling with today is a price level that has continued to rise as long as any living consumer can remember. And this has happened not only in Britain, but also in most other industrialised nations of the world.

Over the years a great deal has been learned about the economy and the reason why it does not function as imagined by the classical economists. It is now all too clear that there is no automatic market mechanism that can be relied upon to keep total demand equal to total supply. Bitter experience has shown that it is possible for the economy to operate at a level far below capacity, leaving large numbers of workers as well as land and capital unemployed. Likewise there can be situations of overemployment—excess demand—in which buyers compete with each other for scarce goods and services, thereby bidding up the price level into an inflationary spiral.

Understanding has led to constructive action. Governments are rapidly learning how to control overall demand and supply in such a way as to keep them roughly in balance. As a result it is possible to claim categorically that severe depression and mass unemployment are gone forever. All political parties are committed to the objective of full employment. The necessary tools have been acquired—and the art is gradually being mastered—of ensuring that the overall level of demand is high enough to provide jobs for all those willing and able to work. The Labour Government is currently taking measures to meet this commitment more completely in certain stagnant areas of the country which have tended to develop regional pockets of unemployment.

Progress has also been made in fighting inflation. Economists have developed a variety of deflationary techniques for "mopping up" excess demand. By and large it has become possible, although far from easy, through taxes and credit restrictions to reduce the total amount of money which people have to spend to just that level which roughly matches the available output. This can prevent a situation of "demand inflation" in which too many buyers are chasing too few goods, and thereby bidding up their prices.

But still prices continue to rise!

Even when there is no "excess demand", there remains a stubborn and chronic problem of inflation. Indeed, prices even rise in the face of unemployed capacity, i.e., when men and machines are idle. This has made it doubly clear that deflation is not the whole answer. The problem is so stubborn that deflation, to be effective, would have to be carried to the point of severe depression and mass unemployment. This is a "solution" which neither governments nor the people are willing to accept—for the simple reason that unemployment and stagnation are far worse than the evils of inflation.

Hence governments and economists are looking for some other kind of remedy. This search has led them to examine more closely the nature of a problem which can no longer be diagnosed merely as "demand inflation" or "buyers' inflation". In looking closer, they have tended to concentrate on what was described earlier as the weakness of the classical approach. This was the assumption that *an individual seller* (whether of a final product, of a raw material, of productive equipment, or of labour) *could not have an influence over the price* at which his product or service would sell.

Every worker, employer and consumer knows that this is no longer true. Indeed, it is doubtful that it was ever true. Certainly in the modern world manufacturers and traders have a great deal of influence over the selling prices of their products and services. They may, as individual firms, have a monopoly, or control a semi-monopolistic share of the total supply. They may combine or conspire or concur with other producers as to what the price shall be. Or they may simply follow the lead of the big fellow with respect to price. The assurance of the government that it will not permit serious unemployment to develop puts a floor under the market. With this under-pinning of demand, sellers know that there is little risk of discouraging buyers by raising their prices—especially since in the prevailing climate of prosperity their competitors are doing the same.

Workers, too, are sellers; wages and salaries are the prices which they charge for their services. And it is now generally recognised that they too have a major influence on what has come to be known as "sellers' inflation" or "cost-push inflation". As individuals, workers cannot influence wages. This is precisely why they joined together into trade unions. At an early date it became all too obvious that no worker on his own could protect his interests against the far greater economic bargaining power of the employer. His only hope to obtain a living wage, to say nothing of a "fair" share of increasing national output, was to pool his strength with other workers in trade unions. Events proved that the struggle to keep up with the cost of living is never finished. Thus necessity became a habit, and it is now accepted as normal for the unions to present an annual claim for wage increases, regardless of the state of the market.

The virtual guarantee of full employment has removed any inhibitions that unions might have had about pricing workers out of a job. And the growing evidence that the fruits of technological progress are seldom channelled to consumers via falling prices has convinced them that it is essential to put forth periodic wage claims through collective bargaining. They see no other way of preventing a decline in labour's share of national output.

A wage increase has to be agreed to by two parties, a worker or his union on the one hand and an employer on the other. In an inflated economy there are several reasons why the employer is not inclined to put up much resistance to wage claims. Because of the shortage of labour he does not want to risk a strike. More important, he need not himself bear the burden of the increased wage costs; he can pass it on to the consumer. In a fully employed economy with steadily rising incomes there is no danger of losing sales as a result of putting up prices. This is particularly true because the seller can be sure that his competitors will also raise their prices to cover their higher wage costs.

Profit margins have remained remarkably stable from year to year. This is clear evidence of the "cost-plus" mentality of employers. Like workers who find it "natural, normal and fair" that they should recoup the losses imposed by a rising cost of living, so employers find it only "natural, normal and fair" that they should increase prices to cover rising costs. But living costs and production costs *always* rise, consistently, year after year. Accordingly both workers and employers have developed attitudes, habits and bargaining institutions to deal with such a situation. These have become deeply woven into the fabric of the economy, and they cannot be changed overnight.

So who started the wage-cost-price spiral? This is as futile a line of enquiry as the proverbial question about the chicken and the egg.

### *Wage Drift*

To a large extent "cost-push" inflation takes the form of wage or earnings "drift"—a phenomenon which is currently attracting a good deal of attention.

#### *What is Drift?*

"Drift" is the difference between the rate of increase in actual earnings received by employees over a given period and the rate of increase in earnings expected as a result of agreements negotiated at national level. These agreements may be between national trade union(s) and employers' association(s), district agreements, arbitration awards at national or district level, or orders by statutory wage-fixing bodies.

#### *What causes Drift?*

Drift assumes many different forms. The amount of drift in a firm depends on the bargaining system, the wage structure, the construction of agreements, and above all on the employer's inclination or disinclination to resist drift.

Careful economic studies have shown that the average drift in a given year is related to the state of the labour market. Drift is noticeably greater when the market is tight, that is, when jobs are chasing workers. This is only natural. It means, for one thing, that workers are not slow to press their advantage as growing labour shortages push up their economic value. Nor are employers inclined to resist these demands. Why should they be? By increasing earnings they can retain their workers and even "lure" some away from competitors. And the process is painless in an "inflation-minded" economy in which it is easy simply to raise prices—as competitors are doing—to cover the added wage costs.

This process of bidding up earnings at the plant level is not at all inhibited by the fact that wages have already been agreed upon by employers and trade unions. There are many ways of increasing earnings without increasing basic rates.

Some of this drift happens automatically as workers move to higher-paid industries, districts or occupations. This pushes up the level of average earnings quite independently of negotiated rates.

There is also the unintentional kind of drift which is legitimate in the sense that it reflects the reward of greater effort. Some of the increases which occur in connection with piecework earnings are of this type, as are genuine special payments for merit, for overtime, or for unusual hardships. This category also includes higher wage levels resulting from genuine productivity bargains as described in Chapter III.

All too often, however, drift is the consequence of inefficient management, undue pressure or "fiddling" by workers or connivance between the two. This "bad" kind of drift may or may not be intentional.

A major source of this kind of drift is what the National Board for Prices and Incomes labels "pieceworkers' creep" in connection with various forms of payment by results.[1]

Piece rates tend over a period of time to yield increasing earnings per unit of "labour input" or effort. One reason for this is that employers find it inconvenient to adjust rates for every small improvement in methods, materials, equipment and organisation. Meanwhile output per man is being increased through faster machines, replacement of tools or materials, minor adjustments on the factory floor, reduction in number of movements, better lighting, improved administration or more efficient issuing of tools and materials.

These continuous small changes add up to significant changes in output and hence in earnings. And if the employer is anxious to make the job attractive to his workers, or if he is subjected to pressure from them, he may see that the rates are set rather "loosely", that is too high, in the first place. Thus the worker reaps the reward for some of the output attributable to other factors of production.

Another factor in drift is the "ratchet" effect described by the National Board for Prices and Incomes.[2] This results from the

[1] *Payment by Results Systems,* National Board for Prices and Incomes, Report No. 65, May 1968, Cmnd. 3627, p. 13.

[2] National Board for Prices and Incomes, *Payment by Results Systems, loc. cit.,* p. 15.

common assumption, in collective bargaining, that new piece rates, times or prices must be fixed so that PBR workers will earn at least as much as in the concluding sequence of their previous tasks. Thus earnings are pushed steadily upward, never down.

Earnings are also increased through many kinds of "incentive" bonuses and special payments. These may be "merit money" in reward for special skills, responsibilities or long service; "machine extras" for work on a particular type of machine or process; "exposure" allowances for work under unpleasant circumstances; or "dirt money", "heat money", "height money" and "wet money". A worker may be "upgraded" into a higher wage bracket—not because of a sudden increase in skill or responsibility, but simply as a way of offering him higher earnings.

*How Much Drift is There?*

Statisticians disagree on the amount of drift even more than they do about most economic measurements. This is because drift can assume so many different forms; and also because it isn't easy to obtain usable data on either basic rates or actual earnings.

The National Board for Prices and Incomes in its recent study on PBR systems described the deficiencies in the existing indices for both (a) rates under national agreements and (b) earnings. Briefly, the Index of Basic Wage Rates or Minimum Entitlements excludes overtime premia, shift allowances, "fall-back" rates or similar guarantees, supplementary allowances for variations from normal working conditions, and holiday payments. And the index for actual average earnings per hour and week includes many factors other than drift; for example, changes in total hours worked or their arrangement, changes in the output of PBR workers and changes in the distribution and composition of the labour force.

Drift is usually calculated by deducting (a) above from (b) and adjusting to exclude the effect of overtime. This yields an annual drift of about *2 per cent a year* for 1963 to 1966.

But the National Board for Prices and Incomes is not satisfied with these results which it regards as an incomplete measure of drift. Hence it decided to make its own estimate, and arrived at a figure for drift of *4 per cent a year,* or twice the official estimate.

The National Board for Prices and Incomes calculations are based upon application of what it calls a "workplace margin" in earnings (except for overtime), that is, earnings over and above nationally agreed basic rates. It believes this margin to be at least one-third and to be increasing; but it is unevenly distributed between sectors and groups.

Striking examples of this "workplace margin" have been cited by the Royal Commission on Trade Unions and Employers' Associations in its report published in June 1968.[1] In October 1967, the "basic"—that is the nationally or regionally agreed—time rate for a normal week of 40 hours for an engineering fitter was £11 1s. 8d. compared to average weekly earnings of £21 7s. 9d. For a building craftsman the comparison was £14 13s. 4d. and £21 13s. 8d.; for skilled shipbuilding and repairing workers £11 1s. 4d. and £21 17s. 8d.; for dock labourers £15 and £22 16s. 6d.; for workers in cocoa, chocolate and sugar confectionery £10 15s. 6d. and £21 7s. 5d.; for electrical cable making £11 8s. 4½d. and £23 9s. 4d.; for furniture manufacturing workers £13 and £22 5s. 4d.; for the motor vehicle retail and repairing trade £11 and £18 10s. 4d.; for soap, candle and edible fat manufacturing £10 6s. 6d. and £23 10s. 5d.; and for footwear manufacturing £11 12s. 6d. and £19 14s. 4d.

*Leapfrogging*

A major feature of drift is its unevenness. It varies: between occupations in a firm; between firms; between different sectors of an industry; and between industries. It is greater for pieceworkers than for time workers, and for male than for female workers. And it tends to be greater for more highly-paid groups, for those who are more effective bargainers, and for workers under managers who tolerate more "looseness" in the setting of rates.

It is this unevenness of drift that causes most of the pressure towards inflation. If earnings drifted upward at the same time and by the same amount for all workers, there would be no reason for

---

[1] Royal Commission on Trade Unions and Employers' Associations 1965–1968, *Report* presented to Parliament, June 1968, Cmnd. 3623, p. 15.

what has come to be known as "secondary drift". This is the fruitless process of trying to restore traditional "relativities", that is, to keep earnings of various groups in the same relationships as they were before the original increases occurred.

Earnings within a firm, within an industry and within an economy are all related to each other in an intricate pattern of differentials. This pattern was never established scientifically. It just evolved as a result of all sorts of historical and accidental developments, and in many cases it no longer fits the current situation. Workers grow accustomed to the fact that group A traditionally earns more than group B, and that group B in turn earns more than group C. They come to feel that this customary pattern is the "fair" pattern. Hence they tend to resist changes in the pattern.

Assume that earnings rise, either through negotiation or through drift, for group A (for instance, engineering workers who often act as pace-setters). This starts a chain reaction. Workers in group B (railway workers) demand a similar rise, either through their trade unions or in plant negotiations via their shop stewards. Group C, in turn (London underground workers followed by busmen in London and then in the provinces) argue that their earnings should go up in step with those for railway workers. By this time some months may have elapsed, and the engineering workers will start asking for further increases pointing to busmen as justification for their demand.

This game, which is fully understandable in terms of "fair shares", has come to be known as "leapfrogging". It is a process that is inevitable in an economy where wages are determined through voluntary bargaining between workers and employers with no limits set as to timing, amount or acceptable grounds for wage claims. But the net result is to perpetuate the inflationary chain reaction of wage–cost–price–wage increases. The impetus stems from the fact that increases in pay packets are unequally distributed; there is considerable unevenness in the impact of collective bargaining.

It is a rare worker who is content to receive a smaller increase than the next fellow. This is particularly so if the next fellow happens to be doing about the same kind of work, or work that is no more strenuous or difficult than his own. So he, or his union, puts in a claim intended to "maintain relativities", or "correct anomalies", or "achieve comparability"; in short, to enable him either to catch up or to regain his previous lead. Thus he "leaps" over the man in front of him in the queue, and the same happens all the day down the line. There is no beginning and no end to the queue; it is always re-forming as the players continue to leap over each other. And it is always moving in the direction of higher wages and higher prices.

### *The Effect of Inflation*

There is wide agreement today that spiralling prices are no longer tolerable. Apart from speculators who thrive on inflation, and the occasional economist or trader who argues that a rising price level is a useful stimulus to business, there are few who are willing to accept the personal injustices and the social and economic distortions which inflation brings with it.

#### *Effect on Individuals*

The chief victims of inflation are workers and their families—that is, the bulk of the population. Workers feel its impact in two ways. One is the frustration involved in the continuing struggle to prevent living standards from being eroded by rising prices. Higher prices mean higher costs of living. Unless wages and salaries are increased in step with rising prices, there will be a decline in "real" wages—that is, the wage packet will be smaller in terms of what it can buy.

Accordingly, workers feel impelled to push for wage increases. This they do through their trade unions via a bargaining process which takes many months. Once accomplished, it must soon be repeated in the face of a new round of price increases as manufacturers try to cover their costs for labour, materials and equipment, all of which have gone up as a result of inflation.

Over the ten years up to 1968 money wages and salaries have risen a little more than 6 per cent a year on average. At the same time the general price level has gone up by about 3 per cent a year. Thus the increase in real wages was less than 3 per cent a year. In short, much of the negotiating effort of workers proved to be in vain. Again and again they were victims of the "great illusion" that they were bargaining for higher standards of living. In the event they always found themselves cheated by about half.

If prices had not moved up, workers' living standards would have risen twice as much. Or if prices had declined as national output expanded—as they are supposed to according to the textbooks—their living standards would have gone up in step with higher productivity. And this would have happened automatically without all the effort involved in collective bargaining.

As it was, wage earners had to keep running to avoid moving backwards. Still they did manage, through sheer persistence and with much wasted energy, to edge slowly forward. But only *on the average*.

The worst evil of inflation is the unevenness of its impact. Within the ranks of workers there are many whose wages lag seriously behind rising prices. Unorganised workers lack the bagaining power to push up their wages in line with living costs. Workers on time rates and in routine clerical and administrative jobs cannot, like production workers, increase their earnings through overtime, piecework and shift bonuses. Earnings in the public sector tend to move up more slowly than in private enterprise. Trade union bargaining strength is relatively weak in declining industries and in stagnant areas of the country.

But the situation is far more desperate for those who live on fixed incomes and have no bargaining channel through which to press for increases. This includes pensioners and widows, the unemployed and those who live on their savings; in short, primarily people in the lower-income brackets. For them there is no remedy, no way of increasing their incomes in step with rising costs of living. They cannot run in order to stay put, but must stand helplessly by as rising prices nibble away at their way of life—by 3 per cent a year on average.

Thus, inflation undermines economic efficiency and political stability by increasing social tensions. The continuing rise in prices inflames the inevitable struggle as to how the national output is to be shared. It embitters pensioners who are helpless before the onslaught on their meagre living standards. It stirs up distrust and hostility between workers in their scramble to keep up one with the other in this struggle. And it widens the gulf between workers and employers as each tries to outstrip the other in the chase after spiralling prices. And in the end inflation also undermines confidence in the government. It creates the impression that those who are supposed to govern are standing idly by, unable or unwilling to protect the victims of rising prices or to repair the damage to economic growth and to international trade and prestige.

*Effect on the Balance of Payments*

Rising prices have a way of plunging the economy into difficulties on the "balance of payments" account. This account has been a chronic source of concern since the war. In recent years Britain appears to have been pricing itself right out of world markets.

Before the war the British regularly and cheerfully imported far more goods and services from abroad than could be paid for from export sales. About one-third of the difference was covered by "invisible" earnings from tourism, shipping, banking and insurance activities and returns from overseas investments. But these sources of finance have since dwindled. Today they take care of only about one-eighth of the trade gap, that is, the excess of imports over exports. At the same time, the flow of capital out of the country has greatly increased as a result of higher military expenditures, expanded aid to developing countries and a larger outflow of private long-term capital.

This puts a heavy and growing responsibility on exports. But these, too, have been faring less well in recent years. Britain's share of world trade in manufactured goods has fallen from 20 per cent in 1955 to 13 per cent in 1965. This was partly because of the slow rate of growth in Commonwealth markets, and partly due to inadequate marketing techniques. But a major reason for this decline has been that British export prices have risen faster than those of many of the countries with which it competes in world markets. The difficulty was that *unit costs* of production were rising faster in Britain.

Changes in unit labour costs reflect changes in labour productivity and in average labour earnings. This is clearly illustrated by data from a recent EEC publication. The following table is a rearrangement of selected data from a tabular presentation in that publication.[1] It ranks countries in terms of increases from 1953 to 1964, from lowest to highest.

| Country | Labour costs per unit output | | Average labour earnings (1953 = 100) | | Labour productivity | |
|---|---|---|---|---|---|---|
| | | Rank | | Rank | | Rank |
| Belgium | 128.1 | 1 | 180.5 | 1 | 142.4 | 2 |
| Austria | 131.2 | 2 | 233.5 | 6 | 177.8 | 8 |
| Norway | 133.5 | 3 | 203.9 | 3 | 150.3 | 5 |
| West Germany | 139.0 | 4 | 220.9 | 5 | 166.3 | 7 |
| Sweden | 141.9 | 5 | 206.7 | 4 | 145.6 | 4 |
| United Kingdom | 144.7 | 6 | 188.2 | 2 | 129.9 | 1 |
| Italy | 149.8 | 7 | 264.0 | 8 | 181.8 | 9 |
| France | 164.3 | 8 | 272.1 | 9 | 165.6 | 6 |
| Netherlands | 171.1 | 9 | 243.9 | 7 | 142.6 | 3 |

This table shows that although only Belgium had a lower rise in average labour earnings than the United Kingdom, the increase in labour productivity in the United Kingdom was far lower than for any of the other countries. As a consequence, British labour costs per unit of output were higher than for five other countries. This makes it clear that the United Kingdom has a strong motivation to find ways of raising labour productivity in order to increase the competitiveness of exports.

Meanwhile imports continue to rise, particularly during the expansion phase of the stop-go cycle when output is pushing against capacity. Imports have to be paid for in one way or another. To the extent that they are not covered by exports and invisible earnings, the government must borrow from abroad. If it borrows too

---

[1] *Incomes in Postwar Europe: A Study of Policies, Growth and Distribution* (Economic Survey of Europe in 1965: Part 2), Chapter 2, page 22, table 2.10.

often and too much, confidence in the pound is weakened, and there is another balance-of-payments crisis.

Such crises have happened again and again in recent years, for example, in 1950, in 1955, in 1960, in 1964, and in 1967. Sterling is particularly susceptible to such crises. This is because the pound has long been used as an "international currency". Throughout the world there are people who hold their capital in the form of sterling, and countries which hold their foreign exchange reserves in sterling. A considerable part of the world's financial transactions as well as the international flow of capital is channelled through London. This means that a great deal hinges on the "soundness" of the pound. Anything that undermines confidence in sterling causes anxiety and concern all over the globe, and leads to an outflow of capital from Britain, thus further straining foreign exchange reserves. In November 1967 the consequence was devaluation of the pound.

*Effect on Economic Growth*

A balance-of-payments crisis is bad enough in itself. Pressure is brought to bear on the government by foreign creditors, Britain's international reputation suffers and capital markets are disrupted. The check to imports puts a strain on the expansion of international trade and also threatens the prosperity of our trading partners.

But the damage done in terms of Britain's economic growth has been even more serious. Since inflation is recognised as a major cause of the balance-of-payments problem, the remedy that is usually prescribed for recurring crises is "deflation"; that is, increased taxes, restrictions on credit, and cuts in government spending in order to reduce overall demand. The intended effect of deflation is that the consumer will have less money to spend; imports will decline; employers will be less willing to grant wage increases; and some workers will lose their jobs and become available, along with unemployed capital and equipment, for work on producing export goods. This is supposed to lead to economic recovery. But in the event it has resulted in long periods of industrial stagnation.

As a result of this "stop-go" reflex there was a long period of stagnation in 1952, in 1957–1958, from mid-1960 to the spring of 1963, and in 1966–1968. The pattern has been graphically presented by the TUC as follows:[1]

| | Output position | Action taken | Cycle 1 | Cycle 2 | Cycle 3 | Cycle 4 | Cycle 5 |
|---|---|---|---|---|---|---|---|
| Phase 1 | begins to pick up* | foot on accelerator | 1948–49 | 1953–4 | 1959 | 1963 | 1968 |
| Phase 2 | top gear† | foot off accelerator | 1950 | 1955 | 1960 | 1964 | |
| Phase 3 | slowing down | brakes | 1951 | 1956 | 1960 | 1965 | |
| Phase 4 | almost stopped | further brakes | 1952 | 1957 | 1961 | 1966 | |
| Phase 5 | stationary | foot taken off brakes | 1952 | 1958 | 1962 | 1967 | |

* unemployment peak
† worst year for balance of payments

The most striking consequence of stop-go is loss of production. When the brakes are applied, demand is curtailed and industry reacts by reducing output far below capacity. At the same time, however, money wages continue to rise. This means rising unit costs, thus offsetting export advantages in foreign markets which might otherwise have resulted from the comparative cost position.

In the expansion phase, although productivity rises rapidly, labour incomes barely keep pace. Profits, on the other hand, grow faster than productivity, rise rapidly and are the major source of rising unit costs. The contrasts are apparent from the following tabulation by the TUC:[2]

[1] *Economic Review* 1968, p. 52.
[2] *Ibid.*, pp. 53, 55.

| Expansion Years | | Years of Stagnation/Slow Growth | |
|---|---|---|---|
| Period | Increase per unit output | Period | Increase per unit output |
| | HOME COSTS | | |
| 1960 over 1958 | 3.2 per cent | 1962 over 1960 | 6.7 per cent |
| 1964 over 1962 | 3.7 per cent | 1966 over 1964 | 7.0 per cent |
| | EMPLOYMENT INCOME | | |
| 1960 over 1958 | 1.1 per cent | 1962 over 1960 | 10.1 per cent |
| 1964 over 1962 | 2.4 per cent | 1966 over 1964 | 9.6 per cent |
| | GROSS PROFITS | | |
| 1960 over 1958 | 7.7 per cent | 1962 over 1960 | -0.1 per cent |
| 1964 over 1962 | 6.6 per cent | 1966 over 1964 | 1.4 per cent |

All of which demonstrates that stop-go and recurrent deflation through monetary and fiscal policies alone do not "solve" the problems caused by inflation. On the contrary, they only interrupt the process of economic growth at a serious cost in wasted resources. It also demonstrates how essential it is for steady economic growth to ensure stability both of unit labour costs and of profits.

## Inflation and Incomes Policy

These were the considerations that led the government in 1964 to launch its prices and incomes policy.

It persuaded the central federations of employers and the TUC to sign a Joint Statement of Intent on Productivity, Prices and Incomes.

It asked trade unions and employers to cooperate voluntarily in holding wage increases within a norm based on expected increases in overall national productivity.

It asked producers and distributors to try to ensure that price increases are "avoided where possible" and prices "reduced whenever circumstances permit".

It undertook a continuing review by the National Economic Development Council (NEDC) of general movements of prices and incomes.

It established a National Board for Prices and Incomes (NBPI) to examine particular increases in prices and wages referred to it by the Government to assess their conformity to the productivity norm.

And it began to issue a steady stream of publicity from NEDC, the "little Neddies" for individual industries, the NBPI, the Department of Economic Affairs, the Ministry of Labour and the Ministry of Technology on the need for increased productivity.

In his May Day message of 1966 the Prime Minister said: "We are still in grave danger of paying ourselves much more than we are actually earning. . . . Unless we hold back on our demands, all our plans for improved industrial efficiency and higher living standards will be undermined."

This statement of the Prime Minister's sums up the inflation paradox which makes a prices and incomes policy so necessary. Why should a push for *higher* incomes result in *lower* living standards? We have seen that this apparent contradiction follows from the attempt of those who have something to sell to push up their incomes too rapidly. If incomes rise at the same rate as total national output, there is no price inflation. If they go up faster than productivity, prices must rise. And a rising price level, because of its uneven impact on individuals as well as its effect on exports and the balance of payments, disrupts productive efficiency, checks economic growth and undermines living standards.

Thus the essence of a prices and incomes policy lies in the attempt to persuade sellers to restrain their demands for higher incomes. In selling their labour, workers must be induced to keep their wage claims within the scope of increased output. And producers and distributors must be induced to refrain from passing on to consumers every increase in costs.

The difficulty of the task lies in the fact that individual sellers—of products or of labour—can be persuaded to refrain from increasing their prices *only if they can be convinced that other sellers are going to do the same.* Without such assurance they would consider themselves stupid to agree—and rightly so.

If a worker were persuaded that all other workers were going to moderate their wage claims, he would not risk his job by putting in a much higher claim. If he were certain that producers were going to keep their prices relatively stable, he would not consider that higher claim to be necessary to counter the higher cost of living.

Similarly, a producer might not risk an increase in his prices if he were convinced that his competitors were going to keep their prices down. Likewise, if he were sure that wages, and hence overall consumer purchasing power, were going to be restrained, he might hesitate to raise prices and jeopardise sales.

By the same token, however, each individual seller knows that if he agrees to wage or price restraint while others fail to do so, he will be the loser. The worker who holds back on wage demands will find his real wages lagging behind those of his colleagues who did not exercise restraint, with the gain from his self-discipline swelling the profits of his employer. And the producer who holds back on price increases will find himself earning lower profit margins than his competitors, and also lower margins than the market will bear. The crux of the problem of operating an effective prices and incomes policy lies in the need for concerted action.

The prices and incomes policy has already gone through a number of phases including an initial "norm" for wage and price increases of 3½ per cent (July 1965 to July 1966); a "standstill" on wage and price increases with very limited exceptions (July 1966 to June 1967); and a period of "nil norm" (July 1967 to March 1968). The current phase, initiated in April 1968, features a ceiling of 3½ per cent on wage, salary and dividend incomes. The only exceptions are for increased productivity or major revisions of wage structure.

Only those increases which satisfy certain criteria specified by the government may be authorised within this ceiling. These criteria are listed in Appendix A. Supervision of increases is made possible through a voluntary "early warning" system of notification and vetting operated with the co-operation of the CBI and the TUC. Notified increases which appear to be in contravention of the prices and incomes policy are referred to the NBPI for careful examination, and the increases are not supposed to take effect pending this review. The government has standing legislative authority to delay increases up to 12 months in the event of reference to the NBPI.

## Productivity Bargaining and the Incomes Policy

The most important of the criteria governing wage increases under the incomes policy is that which relates to productivity. The government has explicitly stated that "priority will continue to be given under the productivity criterion".[1] This criterion provides for increases (up to the 3½ per cent ceiling) "where the employees concerned, for example by accepting more exacting work or a major change in working practices, make a direct contribution towards increasing productivity in the particular firm or industry. Even in such cases some of the benefit should accrue to the community as a whole in the form of lower prices."

The ceiling relates to rates or scales of pay applying to time worked, units of work or output, or a combination of these. It does not apply to earnings which are due to necessary increases in hours worked or in the amount of work done. It covers increases in basic pay rates and allowances, rates for overtime, night or shift working, improvements in fringe benefits, normal or standard hours and holiday entitlement.

Changes in payment by results systems and changes *within* such systems—that is, in piecework rates, bonus rates or standard time —should not result in higher earnings unless they can be justified on grounds of increased effort or other direct contribution towards increasing productivity.

Changes in rates or scales may be settled at national, local, firm or plant level. Where a group benefits from increases or improvements settled at more than one level, the application of the ceiling requires that the *overall* increase should not exceed the 3½ per cent ceiling. In considering increases settled at national level, account must be taken of probable increases at local, company and plant

---

[1] *Productivity, Prices and Incomes Policy in* 1968 *and* 1969, Cmnd. 3590, p. 8.

level. Conversely, increases in rates settled at the plant level should take account of relevant increases at other levels.

*There is one exception to the 3½ per cent ceiling on pay increases, and that is for productivity agreements.*

In the words of the relevant White Paper, "There will be an exception to the ceiling for agreements which genuinely raise productivity and increase efficiency sufficiently to justify a pay increase above 3½ per cent. The guidelines laid down by the NBPI in their Report No. 36 on 'Productivity Agreements' provide the basis for determining the justification for such increases. Major re-organisation of wage and salary structures which can be justified on productivity and efficiency grounds may also qualify for this exceptional treatment."[1]

This exception is certain to have a major impact on the development of productivity bargaining. Already such agreements have been stimulated by the productivity criterion.

> Productivity bargaining, which began as a means devised by management to break through a wall of resistance to changes in entrenched work practices that were designed to restrict output and maximise employment, was at first greeted with hostility and suspicion by the unions, but the limitations on bargaining imposed by the incomes policy since 1964 have greatly changed union attitudes. Many of them now recognise that productivity bargaining provides a legitimate means of increasing pay within the framework of an incomes policy. Attitudes have now changed and there is now a considerable degree of enthusiasm for productivity agreements. In part this is due to the wage restraining policy which can be circumvented by negotiating productivity agreements.[2]

That enthusiasm is likely to multiply now that productivity agreements can be used to justify pay increases above the ceiling.

The NBPI is itself well aware of the implications of the incomes policy for productivity bargaining.

> The rate of growth of productivity agreements will depend in our view upon the maintenance of a prices and incomes policy. All that

---

[1] Cmnd. 3590, p. 9.

[2] B. C. Roberts, *Incomes Policy and Productivity Bargaining,* paper presented at International Conference on Automation, Full Employment and Balanced Economy, Rome, sponsored by the Foundation on Automation and Employment Ltd., 1967.

> we have heard suggests that the effect of Government policy, especially since July 1966, has been to direct the attention of both the employers and trade unionists away from conventional bargaining and towards productivity bargaining. But since productivity agreements require time and effort whereas conventional bargaining is easy, many of them might turn back if the pressure were removed.[1]

It should not be thought, however, that the exception to the ceiling for wage increases in the case of productivity agreements represents an easy way out. As the NBPI says, they require time and effort; and in addition they must satisfy the fairly rigid requirements laid down as guide lines in its report on Productivity Agreements:

> (i) It should be shown that the workers are making a direct contribution towards increasing productivity by accepting more exacting work or a major change in working practices.
>
> (ii) Forecasts of increased productivity should be derived by the application of proper work-standards.
>
> (iii) An accurate calculation of the gains and the costs should normally show that the total cost per unit of output, taking into account the effect on capital, will be reduced.
>
> (iv) The scheme should contain effective controls to ensure that the projected increase in productivity is achieved, and that payment is made only as productivity increases or as changes in working practice take place.
>
> (v) The undertaking should be ready to show clear benefits to the consumer through a contribution to stable prices.
>
> (vi) An agreement covering part of an undertaking should bear the cost of consequential increases elsewhere in the same undertaking, if any have to be granted.
>
> (vii) In all cases negotiators should beware of setting extravagant levels of pay which would provoke resentment outside.[2]

## Summary

Sustained economic growth in Britain has been inhibited by the persistent problem of rising prices which intermittently leads to deflationary measures resulting in what has come to be known as the "stop-go" economy.

A major factor in this inflationary process has been "wage-drift" or the gap between the rate of actual earnings and of the

---

[1] *Ibid.*, p. 40.

[2] NBPI, Report No. 36, *Productivity Agreements,* Cmnd. 3311, pp. 47, 48.

earnings expected as a result of wage rates agreed at national level. Wage drift is largely a result of incentive payments and other wage bonuses at the plant level which are very uneven in their impact as between occupations, firms, industry sectors and types of work. This in turn leads to secondary drift through a process of "leap-frogging" in an attempt to correct anomalies and "restore relativities". Thus the inflationary chain reaction of wage–cost–price–wage increases is perpetuated with its serious consequences for individuals, for social stability, for balance of payments equilibrium and for economic growth.

The government has responded to this problem with its prices and incomes policy, and productivity bargaining has been given an important role in that policy. Wage increases up to the 3½ per cent ceiling are authorised where employees make a direct contribution to increased productivity by accepting more exacting work, or major changes in working practices or major reorganisations of wage and salary structure. And the only exception to the ceiling on pay increases is that granted for genuine productivity agreements.

Chapter III

# Productivity Bargaining and Efficiency in Use of Labour

## Industrial Change and Manpower Utilisation

Technological changes and more complex and minute division of labour bring with them basic changes in the content of individual jobs and the way these jobs should be combined to ensure the most efficient use of manpower.

Modern productive processes are highly integrated and modern machinery and installations enormously costly. Thus it is essential for management to achieve a high degree of control over labour costs. This is necessary to ensure direct savings in labour, flexibility in the use of manpower and the most effective utilisation of expensive capital equipment. All of these require careful planning and coordination.

Any piece of new capital equipment is likely to be more mechanised and highly instrumented than that which it replaces. This in turn alters the content of the jobs associated with it. New skills are required and old ones become obsolete. Wage structures and training are correspondingly affected. Workers must become more interchangeable and capable of a wider range of duties. Manning tables must be revised. Hours must be made more flexible.

Jobs are defined less by their special characteristics and more by their role in the integrated production process. The distinction between white- and blue-collar workers becomes even more blurred. The need for shop floor supervision may diminish as the nature of the production process permits increasing self-supervision; on the other hand, it is equally possible that as the work process becomes increasingly automatic, less initiative is required on the part of the individual worker.

Technological change and larger scale of production also have a marked impact on methods of wage payment. In the nineteenth century it was common for trade unions and employers' federations to negotiate "lists" of piecework prices. These applied right through the industrial sector concerned. But this was only possible because machinery and methods of production were highly standardised throughout an industry.

But mass production and its associated pattern of technology introduced machinery and methods which were particular to a firm, quite unstandardised and continuously changing. This happened first in engineering and then spread to a number of other industries including chemicals, rubber, food manufacturing and light metals. The consequence was that piecework prices had to be adapted to each job in each factory. Most of the old standard piece lists have now been dropped.

Finally, as technological change accelerates, straight piecework becomes less appropriate as a method of wage payment. This is because with increased mechanisation, longer runs and mass production sequences, the amount of output is controlled more by the machine than by the worker. Moreover, machines make it harder to define individual tasks, or to apply simple criteria to the measurement of individual efficiency. And a piecework system is difficult to operate on batch production as in engineering where there may be delays in scheduling work on a wide variety of products in differing quantities.

## Restrictive Work Practices

Much has been written and said about restrictive work practices in Britain. As usual, some of this has been exaggerated.

The exaggeration does not relate to the seriousness of such practices. There is no doubt as to the irrevocable waste and seriously inhibiting effect on economic growth resulting from these brakes on productive efficiency. But what is exaggerated is the tendency to attribute blame primarily to the trade unions, and to look upon productivity bargaining as exclusively a matter of "buying out" offensive trade union practices.

In the pages that follow it should become abundantly clear that restrictive work practices are more often the consequence of concerted action by work groups on the shop floor, or of lax management, than of trade union policy. What should also emerge is the importance of identifying and understanding the motives that give rise to such practices. Only through such understanding can there be effective progress in the task of removing obstacles to productive efficiency.

This implies, first of all, the recognition that there is a reason for every restrictive work practice. As the Royal Commission on Trade Unions and Employers' Associations put it: "All restrictive labour practices have once had some justification."[1]

The underlying motives are, of course, of many different kinds. They do not constitute a single-minded conspiracy to hold up production. But they *do* add up to a serious obstacle to productive efficiency. In the words of William Allen, management consultant for the Fawley productivity agreement: "The manufacturing industries . . . are overmanned, on average, by a factor of two. This means either that (their) present output could be achieved with half the manpower, or that the present manpower could produce an output double that which is now being obtained."[2]

### *Types of Restrictionism*

Restrictive work practices can be roughly classified in five categories: demarcation disputes, overmanning, spurious overtime, restrictions on entry and direct restrictions on output.

#### *Demarcation Disputes*

Most demarcation disputes arise from the introduction of new products, or processes which can be applied by more than one standard craft, or new skill requirements, or the breaking down of the job into several distinct operations which can be done by unskilled workers.

---

[1] *Donovan Report,* Cmnd. 3623, June 1968, p. 77.
[2] "Britain in Blinkers", *Sunday Times,* 12 June 1966.

In recent years demarcation disputes have occurred primarily in the building industry, in vehicles, in ship building and marine engineering, and in metals and engineering.

Examples of such time-wasting squabbles are legion. Here we mention only a few.

In printing, a union may insist that messages must be carried and floors swept by a craftsman. Paper being transferred from one department to another may change hands at a line drawn on the floor. A machine-minder may decline to carry out certain tasks, such as cleaning, on a machine in his care. In other cases he may not be allowed to; for instance where a non-craft union has the traditional right to push buttons on a craft-controlled machine. In the machine room of certain London national newspapers it was found that the machine-minder was in charge of the machine but the brake hand, a member of another union, started and stopped it by pressing a button at a signal from the minder.[1]

On some building sites there are plasterers who won't permit bricklayers to do any cement-faced work where plasterer's tools are required; or joiners to do fibrous plaster work. Slaterers won't let labourers use slate-holing machines. Painters won't let anyone else do preparatory work (priming, lime working, application of tar). In London, paint work must be washed only by skilled labour.[2]

In ship building, plumbers, engineers and coppersmiths argue about who should have responsibility for installing particular kinds of piping. Joiners and upholsterers dispute who should lay linoleum on particular surfaces. Woodworkers, sheet-metal workers and shipwrights contest who should drill holes in aluminium sheet and secure it to wood.[3]

Such quarrels are patently absurd. Yet demarcation disputes are fully understandable as human frictions. Craftsmen have long prided themselves on being the guardians of skills against trespass

---

[1] Royal Commission on Trade Unions and Employers' Associations, Research Papers 4, 1. Productivity Bargaining, 2. Restrictive Labour Practices, 1967.

[2] *Source-book on Restrictive Practices in Britain*, Graham Hutton and Jossleyn Hennessy, Institute of Economic Affairs, 1966.

[3] Royal Commission Research Papers 4, *op. cit.*, p. 61.

by inadequately trained workers. Indeed, at one time they were encouraged in this by employers who were concerned to ensure a steady supply of skilled specialist craftsmen and to maintain quality standards.

But times have changed, and what was once a sensible way of doing a job or splitting up work may have been rendered completely out-of-date by changing technology. "Technological change seems to have been largely responsible for transforming what were once commonsense divisions between crafts into restrictive demarcations."[1]

Meanwhile it is difficult for craftsmen to change with the times. Such changes threaten their job security—in terms not only of actual employment but also of prestige, job satisfaction and level of earnings differentials. Trained craftsmen cannot be expected to welcome the thought of their special skill disappearing, and of the job being done by someone trained only a short time. And they resent being asked to help with process work which they consider "inferior". Every worker wants "a job of his own"—and this is particularly true of craftsmen.

*Overmanning*

This is basically a matter of using more manpower than is actually necessary to get the job done. It takes the form of too many men on a particular machine, or unnecessary use of craftsmen's mates, or requiring skilled craftsmen to stand by for particular functions.

Notable examples have been cited in the various studies made on restrictive work practices. These include the double manning of locomotives, the use of guards on vacuum-braked freight trains; the use of twelve assistants when only six are needed for a battery of twelve printing machines; and insistence on a mate for skilled electricians in electrical contracting. The NBPI noted in the case of railways that if the staff could agree to abolition of traditional demarcation lines, the work of the station and parcel porters at the London main line stations could be done by a third fewer men.

---

[1] *Ibid.*, p. 17.

Flanders has noted[1] that prior to the acceptance of the Blue Book at Fawley there were 300 mates working an average of 3½ hours a day.

Jones and Golding make some trenchant comments on the role of craftsmen's mates. "In some instances the mate in British industry is an unskilled worker who is little more than a bag carrier and tea brewer. . . . The mate's social role is as a prop to the status of the craftsman and the loss of a mate might be regarded by some craftsmen as an indication of down-grading."[2]

Overmanning is sometimes an offshoot of demarcation difficulties where the "solution" has been to insist on continued employment of types of workers no longer needed. A recent example is the case of the British Rail guards. After protracted negotiations, the NUR finally agreed that in return for bonus payments to the guards, guards' vans could be eliminated on freight trains with modern braking systems. But they refused to accept a proposal that the guards, no longer needed on former duties, should be allowed to collect tickets—a proposition which Mr. Greene, the NUR Secretary, described as "doing other people's work".[3]

There was also trouble when British Rail management proposed that the jobs of guards should be merged with those performed by the second member of the footplate crew, the firemen of steam days, thus reducing the number manning a train from three to two. ASLEF objected on the grounds that the seniority of its members on the footplate would thereby be undermined. Guards have traditionally been members of the rival NUR and have had no automatic right of promotion to the footplate.

In shipping, overmanning is known as "welting". This is a deliberate slow-down in order to earn overtime premiums. Half the gang work while the other half take a rest, have a smoke or a cup of tea. It has been estimated that throughout Britain probably fewer than 40,000 dockers would be required for full efficiency as

---

[1] Allan Flanders, *The Fawley Productivity Agreements*, p. 170.

[2] Ken Jones and John Golding, *Productivity Bargaining*, Fabian Research Series 257, November 1966, p. 13.

[3] *Guardian*, 31 October, 1967.

against today's 60,000.[1] Welting is induced by a highly complicated pay structure, and its solution appears to lie in a complete revision of piecework systems.

The problem of overmanning has been neatly summed up by H. A. Clegg:

> Underemployment of labour is one of the major scandals of the British economy. . . . Throughout British industry there must be hundreds of thousands of workers who are paid to do nothing for a considerable part of their working time. Craftsmen's mates are one example; (they are) as much a symbol of the craftsman's prestige as an adjunct to his skill. They wait, perhaps for hours at a time, until the craftsman has something for them to do. Craftsmen themselves stand idle waiting for a member of another craft to perform a job which they could easily do themselves, or soon be trained to do. Then there are the new machines and changes in technology—many of them in use in other countries—which would be introduced here but for limits placed by workers on their output, or "manning" rules governing the number of men to be employed on a given process.[2]

*Spurious Overtime*

The British work more overtime than in practically any other major industrial nation. Only France comes close to the British level.

The latest survey by the Department of Employment and Productivity showed that just over a third of all employees in manufacturing worked an average of about $8\frac{1}{2}$ hours overtime during the week ended 14 December, 1968.[3]

The recent Donovan Report of the Royal Commission on Trade Unions and Employers' Associations points out that although the standard working week has in most industries fallen from 47 or 48 hours in 1938 to 40 in 1967, the average weekly hours actually worked by men fell by only one and a half over this same period. In 1965 their average overtime was running at more than six hours a week, and in some industries such as cement and road haulage it averaged about fifteen.

A good deal of evidence has accumulated to show that much of this overtime is unnecessary. Workers spin out jobs in order to

---

1 *Financial Times*, 30 October 1967.

2 *Socialist Commentary*, December 1964.

3 *Loc. cit.*, p. 24.

obtain the premium rates paid for overtime. Such premiums have become an integral part of the pay packet.

Flanders has characterised this kind of systematic unnecessary overtime as "overtime which, by being permanently maintained at a high level has become built into the firm's wage structure, labour policy and work habits".[1]

Lorry drivers, for example, try to put in eleven hours a day for five to six days a week, and bakery workers sometimes work as much as 20 hours overtime a week or more. The NBPI noted that in both railways and in baking, arrangements have been made between employers and trade unions that are designed to maintain earnings rather than meet the requirements of production. The electricity supply industry is noted for "policy overtime" intended to make earnings competitive with those in manufacturing. In this industry there are sometimes as many hours worked overtime as in a normal working week.

There are a number of factors which explain the prevalence of excessive overtime in Britain. There is very little statutory control over hours, and most collective agreements leave the issue to be determined at the work place.

At plant level various pressures combine to create a permissive attitude as far as overtime is concerned. There are always some workers who are willing, indeed eager, to work long hours in order to swell their pay-packets. This is most frequently the case where average earnings are low. The evidence shows that much overtime is used to compensate for low hourly rates. Understandably this development is not discouraged by local trade union representatives.

Excessive overtime is also in large part a result of management inertia. First line supervisors are not anxious to disturb the harmony of the work shop by exercising more rigorous control over hours. This is particularly true when *their* earnings depend in part on the level of earnings of overtime workers.

Nevertheless, recent experience shows that it is usually possible to reorganise hours and the flow of work in such a way as to obtain the necessary effort without overtime.

---

[1] *Op. cit.*

*Restrictions on Entry*

Some unions, particularly craft unions as in the printing industry, limit the number of apprentices permitted each year in an attempt to keep wages high by sustaining the scarcity value of the skill. The Donovan Report states:[1]

> We have had evidence from a number of sources of obstacles being placed in the way of the employment as skilled workers of persons trained at government training centres. The Engineering Employers' Federation said, for example, that in the Manchester area officials of the Amalgamated Engineering Union refused to allow such persons to be employed as skilled men even if registered as dilutees; and that the union's Tyne district committee adopted the same attitude. Trade union opposition to placing of such persons in skilled work was alleged to exist also in Scotland. The Ministry of Labour's evidence confirmed that government training centres met difficulties of this kind.

A closely related practice is the imposing of restrictions on upgrading, in an effort to protect craft status and skill differentials. In the printing industry, for example, the NBPI found that it is difficult, and sometimes impossible, for machine assistants to graduate to become machine-minders no matter how much skill they acquire. In one case there was an annual quota for probationers to be accepted for upgrading over a period of three years.

*Restrictions on Output*

Sometimes workers set fixed limits for output on various machines and other operations, such as packing parcels, that are well below the average that could reasonably be expected. In other cases fixed times are set for jobs like oiling and cleaning machines without regard to the time actually needed on the particular machine. In oil distribution limits have been set on the speed of vehicles. Sometimes it is even the average overall journey speed that is limited. For example, heavy goods vehicles may average 30 miles an hour where the legal limit is 40 miles per hour.

The Royal Commission on Trade Unions and Employer Associations cited startling practices in London newspapers. In the composing room, no pieceworker started work until there was enough

---

[1] *Op. cit.*, p. 89.

copy to enable every operative present to be issued with the equivalent of 12 lines of setting; hence 20 or 30 operatives might wait until copy became available for the last one. And in the machine room, machine running speeds were negotiated at a level well below the capability of the equipment and in many cases the actual running speeds were lower than the negotiated speeds.

Similarly, T. Lupton found in heavy electrical engineering that workers when being time-studied by the rate fixer took care not to work too fast, and if necessary sought the shop steward's help in seeing that rates were not fixed too tightly.[1]

As Lupton emphasises, the motives underlying such restrictions are the beliefs of workers that they are in this way preventing the cutting of piece rates, stabilising their incomes and achieving a degree of control over the relationship between effort and reward.

*Work Group Sanctions*

W. E. J. McCarthy, Research Director of the Royal Commission on Trade Unions and Employers' Associations, argues that strikes are only the "most extreme and immediate form of workshop sanction in the hands of shop stewards and their members". He has described a whole range of other sanctions which are applied as tactics in the informal "bargaining" strategy of work groups.[2] For example, there are "downers" which are short strikes of a few hours' duration to force assurances that a particular problem will receive immediate attention. There are bans on overtime, "laying back on the job", and wasting management's time with unimportant grievances. Or workers and their stewards can "put on the heat" by withdrawing their usual cooperation and "helper functions"; by insisting on certain formal rights under collective agreements that are normally ignored; or through spasmodic "go slows" and minor output restrictions.

McCarthy suggests that the motive for many of these sanctions is to strengthen the relative bargaining position of work groups with respect to the settlement of grievances in the shop. At the

---

[1] Royal Commission Research Paper 4, *op. cit.*, p. 64.

[2] Royal Commission Research Paper 1, *The Role of Shop Stewards in British Industrial Relations*, 1966, pp. 21–24.

same time he is careful to point out that management, too, sometimes employs similar tactics to strengthen its bargaining power. " . . . workers have no monopoly of sanctions. Managers can suddenly become less cooperative and unwilling to concede even the most insignificant claim. They can demand their rights under an agreement and seek to tighten up on facilities which they have previously granted to the stewards. They can authorise more strict supervision, demand more output, clamp down on unauthorised breaks and declare war on all kinds of accumulated privileges."[1]

In summary, restrictive work practices appear to be motivated by several factors, including worker quest for security.

> The fears associated with change are reasonable fears. For change may face people—and their families too—with urgent practical problems. Technological change, the expansion of new industries and the decay of old, and the need for mobility of labour mean that men are obliged to change jobs, and perhaps to move to completely new areas to live and work. They may find the skills they possess are no longer in demand. They may face a severe cut in pay, and so on. These are substantial problems and so long as they go unsolved the introduction of change itself will be held up.[2]

—tradition

> "Some have become fossilised in union tradition or working rules despite having lost their justification long ago."[3]

—lax management

> Over a long period of time, when the pressure has been great enough, employers have been willing to concede to unions that they have the right to regulate the entry of workers to a particular occupation and to determine how those workers shall be employed. . . . Under conditions of full employment and serious shortages of labour, employers have retreated still further. They have surrendered the right to decide how work shall be carried out and by whom to a greater degree than in any other advanced industrial country.[4]

—and the influence of work groups attempting to increase their bargaining strength.

> In any given situation groups of workers will have shared interests which they will wish to preserve. . . . In this it must be understood that work groups' motives are not negative—they do not set out to

---

[1] *Op. cit.*, pp. 23–24.
[2] *Donovan Report, loc. cit.*, p. 77.
[3] Flanders, *op. cit.*, p. 236.
[4] Roberts, *op cit.*

prevent management succeeding; rather their objective is the quite rational and positive one of promoting their own interests.[1]

Also it should be stressed that the majority of restrictive work practices are not imposed by trade union rule; they stem much more from custom or local initiative at the work shop.

## Productivity Bargaining and the Use of Labour

The productivity agreements concluded so far have incorporated at least one and usually more of the following kinds of change designed to increase efficiency in the utilisation of manpower: greater flexibility of the work force; changes in the time pattern of work; and changes in methods of wage payment.

A rough idea of the relative incidence of the changes incorporated into productivity agreements is provided by an analysis made by the Department of Employment and Productivity of approximately 200 cases involving changes in working practice.

| Type of change | Number of cases in which change occurred |
|---|---|
| 1. *Quantity of Work*<br>e.g., speeding up of machinery or track, elimination of tea breaks, etc., elimination of restrictions on output. | 144 |
| 2. *Nature of Work*<br>e.g., greater flexibility between crafts and job enlargement. | 88 |
| 3. *Rearrangement of Working Hours*<br>e.g., changes or elimination of overtime, introduction of new shift patterns. | 61 |
| 4. *Manning*<br>e.g., reduction of numbers employed, elimination of mates. | 81 |
| 5. *Organisation*<br>e.g., introduction of new supervision structures, setting up of new work groups. | 18 |
| 6. *Change of Methods*<br>e.g., by introduction of method/work study. | 95 |
| 7. *Responsibility*<br>e.g., more share in decision making by work people. | 5 |

[1] Royal Commission Research Papers 4, *loc. cit.*, p. 51.

*Greater Flexibility of the Work Force*

Most productivity agreements have made some attempt to increase the *interchangeability* of workers among the various tasks to be done. The objective is to increase mobility between crafts, beween crafts and non-crafts, and even between departments within a plant. This involves assigning individual workers a wider range of duties. Many different ways of accomplishing this have been devised in connection with productivity agreements.

1. One method is the *general statement of intent*. Management makes an agreement with the unions concerning the need for more flexibility and better use of manpower and the intention of both sides to work towards removal of limitations on the deployment of labour. The Electricity Council signed this kind of agreement, leaving it to plant managers to implement it with specific arrangements after the agreement came into force.

A more effective refinement of this approach was adopted by ICI. Its agreement laid down general principles outlining five different ways in which limitations on deployment of labour were to be removed. At the same time, however, "teeth" were added through a requirement that the new higher rates of pay offered in return for greater flexibility would apply only in plants which had worked out the detailed application of these general principles.

2. The opposite approach is to work out a *detailed list* of the specific job functions involved in plant operations and the changes required in the interest of greater craft flexibility. At Fawley, craftsmen were still designated by their particular trade, but it was specified that certain jobs could be done by two, three or even four crafts. At Coryton Mobil, craft jobs were broken down into 70 carefully specified tasks each of which could be undertaken by two or more crafts. A variation was introduced at Shell's Petrochemicals plant at Carrington where some 43 tasks were listed which were to be performed only by a specific craft, with the stipulation that all others would be interchangeable subject to time, tools and ability. Esso Distribution worked out fairly detailed job descriptions for drivers and plant operatives; similarly the Spencer steel

works prepared detailed job descriptions which permitted tasks to be performed by more than one craft.

There are advantages and drawbacks with both the general intent and the detailed listing approaches. Managers tend to be sceptical of the former; they feel that too much is left to choice. On the other hand, this approach has the virtue of putting more of the responsibility on plant managers for working out details in the light of local circumstances. The "listing" method is not easy to apply because of the difficulty of defining a "normal" job in view of the great variety of processes and techniques, and of constant changes in them.

There is also the danger that in "pricing" separately each item of desired change, rigidity will be introduced, changes will be limited to only those specified and there will be undue stress on a "shopping list" or "buying out" rather than on "gain-sharing". Much will depend on the attitudes of the two parties to the agreement. Perhaps the most useful comment in this connection is that of Jones and Golding: "The effectiveness of both approaches is directly related to the quality of the previous industrial relations and the methods used in negotiating the agreement."[1]

3. At Alcan it was agreed that each worker should have a normal job but be prepared to do other specified tasks for which he was qualified.

4. Many agreements have transferred craft jobs to non-craft workers and also permitted craft workers to do some non-craft work. At ICI, for example, some of the less skilled craft tasks subsidiary to the work of production operatives can now be performed by them; support work for craftsmen can be done by anyone; and in some circumstances "tradesmen" will be expected to operate plants and to do the work of other tradesmen when it is a subsidiary part of their own job. And at Milford Haven the ultimate aim is virtually complete craft/process flexibility, with both craft and operating grades being replaced by the one grade of refinery technician.

---

[1] Jones and Golding, *loc. cit.*, p. 13.

5. In many productivity agreements the reduction in the number of mates has been closely associated with efforts to achieve greater flexibility. In some cases mates have been partially (Post Office) or completely eliminated (Alcan and Spencer), and craftsmen are required either to take over their jobs or to work in groups of two or more. Sometimes personal mates are replaced by "pools" of mates available when and where needed. Many agreements have provided for upgrading of displaced mates.

6. Most of the agreements state explicitly that craftsmen will be prepared to be supervised by employees who do not belong to their own craft. In some cases this has only been extended to other craft supervisors, but at Milford Haven and Carrington, craftsmen, if necessary, work under the supervision of process supervisors. At the same time there has been a streamlining of the supervisory structure resulting in the elimination of the grade of charge-hand and more emphasis upon self-supervision.[1]

*Introduction of a More Effective Time Pattern*

*Overtime* is a key issue in the majority of productivity agreements. Moreover, it is frequently the starting point. This is because reduction in the number of work hours necessitates reorganisation of shift patterns, greater inter-craft flexibility and changes in the level and structure of pay to compensate for loss of overtime premium payments.

"It would appear that as long as there is no decrease in the total amount of work or increase in the labour force, the reduction of overtime working offers the greatest single initial contribution productivity bargaining can make to the efficient utilisation of the labour force in the British economy."[2]

The attack on overtime has been mounted in different ways. In Electricity Supply, overtime premia were virtually eliminated through a complicated system of stagger patterns including a standard week with no overtime for 7 days, or 6 days, or staggering

---

[1] Jones and Golding, *op. cit.*
[2] *Ibid.*

of hours over any 4 or 5 days of the week, or a work week that fluctuates with the seasons or with changes in work load. The same result was obtained at Mobil Oil by providing that any overtime which had to be worked should be paid for not in money but in time off.

Some agreements have achieved significant reduction in overtime by setting targets, often combined with reorganisation of the pattern of shifts. The target for Esso Distribution was to reduce overtime to 5 per cent of working time annually; for Alcan 2 per cent; and at Fawley 6 per cent for process workers and 2 per cent for maintenance workers.

Plant by plant limits were imposed by Shell (up to 200 overtime hours a year) and at Mobil (40 or 44 hours a week). British Oxygen imposed uniform percentage cuts at each plant.

Since overtime premia have been such an important component of wage packets, there has been a good deal of resistance to cuts in overtime. But once the change is made, it is usually gratefully accepted by both sides. "The whole pattern of social behaviour has been altered and the encouraging feature is that there is evidence that once men have broken the habit of excessively long hours and their take-home earnings have not decreased, there is considerable reticence on their part to undertake overtime work."[1]

Although the new arrangements have reduced take-home earnings in some cases—but not many—they have at the same time increased stability of earnings. This, in turn, has provided a more stable basis for compensation claims, sick pay, holiday pay, house mortgages and hire purchase contracts. And of course the average work week has been dramatically reduced for those concerned; in some cases the reduction has been as much as 20 per cent.

### *Changes in Methods of Wage Payment*

A contract of employment between an employer and an employee provides that a certain amount of work—in terms of output or of time—shall be done in return for an agreed payment (including

---

[1] Jones and Golding, *op. cit.*, p. 28.

fringe benefits as well as wages or salary). Clearly, what has to be done for the payment is as important a part of the agreement as the payment itself.

And yet, until recently only wages were bargained about collectively between employers and trade unions. By and large, decisions on pay were divorced from decisions about organisation and conditions of work because the latter were considered to be matters for unilateral managerial decision. True, many agreements on work were reached at plant level between management and workers, but these were kept informal and undocumented. They were not brought into the framework of collective bargaining.

Productivity bargaining, however, has changed all this. The essence of productivity bargaining is the negotiation between trade unions and the employer of an agreement which links changes in work with changes in payment.

One reason this has happened is that employers, trade unions and the government have recognised that systems of wage payment are important instruments for controlling the efficiency of a firm.

Incentive wage systems can provide a major stimulus to increased output. And the development of appropriate wage systems and structure can save administrative time, endless disputes and friction between workers, and between supervisors and workers. It can also alter the restrictive "go-slow" attitude of workers who are dissatisfied with the norms emerging from inappropriate systems or who fear adverse changes in those norms. This is accepted by trade unions. Workers like wage incentives, but they also want stability, predictability and a system that is easy to understand. In short, they want security.

They also want equity. If workers can be convinced that changes in systems of wage payments will eliminate anomalies and result in more rational and objective wage structures, they will be more cooperative.

Finally, changes in wage structure can be a help in increasing flexibility of the work force by eliminating differentials between craftsmen and other groups and removing obstacles to mobility of workers between different occupations and locations.

*Payment by Results (PBR)*

1. *Definitions*

Although the underlying principles of various systems of payment by results are basically simple, they have attained a high degree of technical complexity in application. Hence it may be useful to provide a short glossary of definitions largely derived from the report on Payments by Results Systems of the NBPI.[1]

"Straight piecework": a money price per unit of output so that earnings vary in proportion to amount produced.

"Time-based piecework": effort is calculated not in terms of physical output, but of time. The worker is paid on a basic time rate; a standard time is set for the job and a bonus is paid in relation to time saved in actual performance or extra output in time allowed.

"Geared piecework": the price per unit of output varies at different levels of production.

"Regressive piecework": effective price per unit declines as worker's output rises.

"Commission piecework": price is a fixed percentage of turnover or sales.

"Lieu bonuses": pay for "indirect" workers (engaged in ancillary occupations such as maintenance) based on average bonus of "direct" workers (who perform some operation on the product itself).

"Measured day work": time rate payment but with work-loads fixed by work study.

"High day rates": time rates based on maintenance of high standards of output.

"Stepped" or "graduated" measured day work: different fixed levels of performance rewarded with appropriate levels of pay.

"Rucker" and "Scanlon" bonus systems: based on calculation of a "norm" for the wage bill as a proportion of added value or output value. If payroll costs are later reduced as a proportion of

---

[1] *Loc. cit.*

this value, the difference between the norm and the actual proportion is shared out as a bonus.

"Merit bonus": reward for long service, or good timekeeping, or good quality of product, or high performance or aptitude.

### 2. *Extent of Payment by Results*

The proportion of British wage earners in all industries paid by results rose from 25 per cent in 1938 to about 32 per cent in 1951, and had risen to 33 per cent in April 1961 (42 per cent for manufacturing), the date of the latest enquiry by the Ministry of Labour. This means that PBR applies to at least 4 million workers. At that time, 30 per cent of men employed were paid by results and 44 per cent of women. Seventy-three per cent of all workers in manufacturing were in plants where some workers were paid by results. This means that they may be subjected at least indirectly to the system by means of lieu bonus or "comparability" bargaining.

Engineering, shipbuilding and vehicle manufacture account for over 40 per cent of the male PBR workers in manufacturing. The TUC estimates that more than half of the manual workers in these industries are paid by results.

### 3. *Pros and Cons of Payment by Results*

Payment by results is likely to persist at a fairly high level for some time to come in Western Europe, and even in the United States because it has become traditional as a way of life. Workers see it as a means of increasing their earnings, of rewarding variations in capacities, and of retaining some freedom of choice as to pace of work. Management sees it as a way of stimulating output. And supervisors see it as relieving them of the need to prod workers.

So long as there is still some possibility of worker influence over the pace and method of work—that is, so long as these are not completely and automatically controlled by the production process —there will be a place for payment by results.

*But,* as noted in the NBPI study on PBR, the system is only appropriate where:

—work is measurable and directly attributable to the individual, that is, where it is manual, repetitive, in fairly short-cycle operations;

—the pace of work is controlled by workers rather than by the machine or the process;

—management is capable of maintaining a steady flow of work, and of absorbing short-term fluctuations in demand or output; and

—tasks are fairly constant through time, and not subject to frequent changes in methods or materials or equipment.

However, the list of *cons* culled from a wide number of studies on the subject is considerably longer than that of the pros:

—Piece rates are unrealistic since increasingly output is governed by the pace of the machine and is not subject to worker control.

—There is no objective way of fixing piece rates; they are often decided by "jobbing back" to a subjective assessment of what a reasonable rate of earnings would be.

—The effect of piece rates on output tends to "decay" with the passage of time.

—Piece rates hamper mobility within the firm because workers on a high rate are unwilling to move to jobs in which rates might be "tighter".

—The system creates anomalies in earnings differentials unrelated to genuine effort and skill.

—Piece work creates instability in individual earnings.

—Piece rates encourage restrictive working practices, resistance to new productive methods, and group pressures to "go slow", "fiddle" or penalise "rate busters", thus disturbing the relations between effort and output. Similarly with "cross booking", where a part of the time saved on "loose" jobs is not declared in the time sheets, but is "banked" and then "booked" into tight jobs to stabilise earnings and protect against rate-cutting. Because of the subjectivity of rate-setting, it is natural that workers attempt to manipulate incentive schemes. This is a process of compromising between different ideas of a fair day's work and adjustment by workers to inaccuracies and inconsistencies in rating and programming. Moreover, supervisors, rate-fixers, inspectors and other management representatives at shop-floor level are often under pressure from groups of workers to help them maintain the standards they have set. What is involved is a complex system of social relations, involving mutual rights and obligations.[1]

—Output may be stimulated at the cost of quality or care of materials and machines.

—PBR systems are expensive to install and operate and can be costly in terms of payroll if management loses control of rate setting.

—Unless the system is simple and intelligible it will be difficult for workers to understand and therefore will lose its incentive effect.

—Piece work undermines confidence between workers and management and engenders friction, disputes over rates and unofficial strikes.

—Piece rates waste management time in clerical work, in negotiations over rates and in unofficial strikes. In one firm cited by the NBPI every £100 paid in bonus cost £45 in administrative expense.

—Piece work encourages lax supervision by leaving the responsibility to the individual workers.

—Payment by results is a major source of wage drift, leapfrogging and inflation. Under the guise of "incentive bonuses", these extra payments have been used by employers as a lure in competing for workers in a tight labour market. But, as with many competitive devices, the temporary relative advantage to a particular employer is lost as similar lures are adopted by competitors. What remains is a wider gap between basic rates and actual earnings, a decided bias towards wage drift, and a complex and chaotic jumble of payments systems which bear less and less relation to genuine effort and increased worker efficiency. In short,

---

[1] Tom Lupton, *Money for Effort,* No. 11, Problems of Progress in Industry, Department of Scientific and Industrial Research, 1961.

payment by results has had the effect of stimulating the use of wage comparisons in collective bargaining and at the same time undermining the reliability of those comparisons.

*Work Study and Job Evaluation*

In *theory* a PBR system ensures the "rate for the job". It guarantees that identical effort put forth in work of a given skill and description is rewarded by the same earnings wherever that system is in use.

In *practice,* however, rate determination in connection with PBR is a bargaining proposition. As the Donovan Report says, "prices are fixed by bargaining methods often described as those of a Persian market". Too much depends upon the negotiating skill of particular shop stewards and particular supervisors or specialist rate-fixers.

This is why attention is currently being focussed on work study and job evaluation as a means of introducing more objectivity into the wage structure. The NBPI defines "work study" as a combination of "methods study" and "work measurement".

"Methods study" is a comprehensive analysis of the production in the work shop situation and all of the factors influencing worker output. This should be the first step in working out a rational wage system, but unfortunately it is frequently omitted.

The next stage, "work measurement" involves: measuring the time taken to perform a specified task (in the older systems of work study this is done with a stop-watch); "rating" the effort of the worker being measured to determine whether his performance represents a reasonable norm; and setting a standard based on the time and the rating plus agreed allowances for rest pauses, personal needs, unavoidable delays, etc.

The result of "work measurement" is a standard for the normal effort expended in a given time at a given task. To translate this into terms of money for purposes of devising the wage structure it is necessary to match all the norms with cash rewards. This process is known as "job evaluation".

The purpose of "job evaluation" is to set a rate for a job irrespective of the attributes of individual workers who may be employed on the job in order to establish the rate for one job in relation to another. As the TUC explains,[1] "job evaluation" does not take account of what individual workers can do, given adequate opportunity and incentive. It is concerned with rates and differentials insofar as these depend on inherent requirements of jobs like skill, physical demands and responsibility. Individual performance in meeting the demands of the job is taken care of by PBR bonuses and/or by "merit rating".

There are various methods of job evaluation. The simplest is "ranking" jobs in order of importance on the basis of job descriptions and then ascribing money rates to each. The "classification" method determines the number of wage grades to be used—frequently 5 or 7; draws up a specification for each grade; establishes appropriate rates of pay for each; and then assigns actual jobs to the category with which they most nearly conform. The more elaborate system of "points rating" involves preparation of complete job descriptions in terms of work content and requirements; devising a set of assessment "factors" and assigning a range of points to each; and combining the results of these two stages to determine the points value of each job and hence its relative position in the wage structure. A more complicated variant of this system is known as "factor comparison".

As the NBPI points out,[2] "work-studied incentive bonus systems have the great advantage over ordinary piecework that money values are not negotiated with each task; *a money rate is agreed on for a standard effort expended in a given time,* and this remains constant while tasks change." (Italics added.)

But even work-studied rates are not completely objective. There are still elements of personal judgement involved, and still room for supervisors and work groups to influence the outcome. For example, the work study technician compares the pace of the worker he is studying *with what he conceives to be a "normal" performance.* And determination of the "allowances" for rest and delays is necessarily arbitrary.

---

[1] *Job Evaluation and Merit Rating,* 1964.

[2] Report on Payment by Results Systems, *loc cit.,* p. 50.

These problems have led to the development of a number of newer, more "scientific" methods of work study and measurement. Basically they involve the use of "synthetic" times or of "predetermined" times.

Synthetic times are records of times for tasks or job elements which have been established and accepted by workers and employees in the past, thus increasing the consistency of the measurements used. The NBPI suggests[2] the possibility of pooling the "data banks" of this kind of information which has already been collected by individual firms through "data bank consortia" which could be made available to all firms.

"Predetermined" times are values for jobs which are read off a predetermined scale of standard rates for elements. There are various types of "predetermined motion-time systems (PMTS)" of which the best-known are "Methods Time-Measurement" (MTM) and "Work-Factor". They are all based on the assembly of a catalogue of the manual-motion and mental-process times for *every movement* involved in a work situation. These time values have been measured over extensive periods not by stop-watch but by special measuring instruments, cameras and photo-electric timing devices. From this catalogue of predetermined times for elemental motions the total time can be calculated for total tasks and entire jobs.

Lupton has indicated how these newer PBR systems increase managerial control. Traditional systems of PBR leave workers free to make individual or collective decisions about the relationship between effort and reward. This in turn makes it difficult to set standards and plan work programmes. But the newer systems offer regular weekly amounts of pay in return for consistent levels of measured performance. Payment is not *directly* related to pieces of output or time saved. Rather there is a contract in which the individual worker undertakes to maintain a certain pace of work in return for a weekly wage. This differs from time work which offers no guarantee of pace. Also it requires management to ensure the flow of work. It is sometimes possible for some workers to earn more by working faster.

---

[2] *Ibid.*, p. 51.

Moreover, such methods are far superior to the older stop-watch systems of work study in terms of consistency and thoroughness. But as Lupton points out, they are more accurate only in the sense that the *errors are standard*.

There is an even more serious obstacle to complete "objectivity" in the process of job evaluation. This is the inherent difficulty of assigning weights to the various qualities—skill, memory, physical effort, responsibility, supervision, working conditions, etc.—of which "job content" is comprised. It is easy enough to define such qualities in terms of job descriptions, but any attempt to rank them, that is, to assign priorities for purposes of wage differentials, is necessarily subjective. The exercise can be done more or less arbitrarily by seeking the consensus of experts, but at best there will always be room for argument.

Another problem relates to the hostility of many workers to work study and job evaluation. Their suspicions are based upon past experience with the use of job evaluation and time and motion studies as devices for speeding up work tempo without corresponding increase in earnings. They also fear that it may be used as a rationale for down-grading workers. This no doubt explains the observation in the NBPI report on Railway Pay[1] that "although the trade unions at national level have accepted in principle the adoption of work study schemes in the main workshops, there has been no general implementation of such schemes, because local committees will not accept their application to particular shops."

This distrust on the part of workers is understandable. But there is a good chance that it can be gradually dispelled. The TUC insists that job evaluation schemes should be kept firmly within established negotiating arrangements. It is a function of trade union officials to insist on joint negotiation and consultation and to maintain a constant "policing" of job evaluation systems in order to ensure adequate definitions and descriptions of jobs and correct selection of factors and the relative weights given them.

---

[1] National Board for Prices and Incomes, Report No. 8, *Pay and Conditions of Service of British Railways Staff,* Cmnd. 2873, January 1966.

If workers know that their representatives have participated in the working out of, and the control over, work study methods and job evaluation, they are more likely to accept that the results are not going to be used against them.

In the Carreras tobacco firm, consolidated rates were introduced as part of a broad scheme covering the various groups of workers, clerks, salesmen and junior management as well as different classes of manual workers. The allocation of jobs to various grades was done through an evaluation carried out jointly by management and union representatives.

The NBPI has made the point that work measurement should be "scrupulously insulated from bargaining pressures" through a clear separation of work study from the final fixing of time or price; hence that work study engineers should deal only with foremen and not directly with workers.[1] Such "insulation" may be desirable. But it is important that it should not be interpreted to exclude participation in work study and rate fixing by trade union representatives who have been carefully trained in work study and job evaluation techniques.

*Relevance of Methods of Wage Payment to Productivity Bargaining*

The NBPI considers work study to be a key feature of the effort to achieve more efficient use of manpower. In one of their earliest reports[2] they stated: "We regard work measurement as an indispensable tool to management in assessing what should be the proper deployment of labour."

And in the recent report on Payment by Results Systems[3] the Board pointed out that: "Our investigations have shown that workers are as concerned with the equity and stability of earnings as they are with their absolute amount, and are therefore likely to be willing to 'trade off' those features which permit a rapid and uncontrolled rise in earnings in exchange for alternative advantages."

---

[1] Report on Payment by Results Systems, *loc. cit.*, p. 52.
[2] Report No. 8.
[3] Report No. 65, p. 29.

In that same report the Board recalled that major reorganisation of wage and salary structures which can be justified on grounds of productivity and efficiency can qualify as an exception to the $3\frac{1}{2}$ per cent ceiling under the prices and incomes policy. Accordingly they suggest[1] that managers responsible for payments systems should consult the Board's guidelines for productivity agreements whenever they contemplate a change from conventional PBR to an alternative system such as measured daywork or the introduction of a new PBR system.

The report went on to point out that the main problem in connection with PBR is to determine how far existing PBR systems are working in accordance with the aims of the incomes policy. To aid management in this effort they present a detailed list of guidelines to be used to guage the health of a PBR system. These are reproduced in Appendix B.

Finally, the Board concluded this phase of its report with the following observations which seem to underline the relevance, in its view, of methods of payment to productivity bargaining.

"We recommend the general use of formal work study, and particularly synthetic or predetermined measured time systems, rather than simple rate fixing. We also favour the use of times rather than piecework prices for standard setting. . . . Work study should be made part of the whole system of production control. and . . . it should operate with a clearly-defined and jointly-negotiated set of 'ground rules'. . . . We conclude that where the existing industry-level machinery is inadequate for the negotiation of such ground rules, they are the proper subject for plant or enterprise agreement. Our aim is not to weaken collective bargaining, but rather to replace the present fragmented workplace bargaining by negotiation through representative bodies at a level where the full effects of PBR earnings can be taken into account."[2]

Work study and measurement and revision of pay structures have played an important role in the productivity agreements so far concluded. Nearly every productivity agreement contains clauses relating to the acceptance of work study.

---

1 *Donovan Report,* p. 64.
2 *Ibid.,* p. 57.

Another feature common to most productivity agreements has been reduction in the number of pay grades in the interest of flexibility. Notable examples are Alcan (where over forty rates were reduced to seven grades), ICI, Esso Distribution and the other oil distribution agreements.

The principle involved is well illustrated by the ICI agreement. Here the company stressed the need to adapt pay systems to technical change, since in its view the incentive bonus scheme had gradually lost its relevance and its continued use on an increasing number of jobs in which there is less relation between output and effort had distorted the pay structure. The unions, too, expressed their dislike of the incentive bonus scheme because it created inequities and fluctuations in pay.

Accordingly, the main improvement was to assign each worker to one of eight annual salary levels on the basis of the results of job evaluation. "The graded salary structure indicates the effect of applying the flexibility principle. Job evaluation takes account of the extensions of skill and responsibility in the determination of the appropriate salary level so that willingness to accept greater flexibility is rewarded. Moreover, all workers irrespective of their degrees of skill are in the same salary structure. Differentials are rationalised and opportunities for higher pay as a result of accepting movement from one job to another are created."[1]

Many productivity agreements have also stressed the *consolidation* of special payments with basic rates in order to reduce confusion in the wage structure and achieve greater stability of earnings.

A typical example is the steel industry where "it is possible to encounter every type of abnormal working conditions—extreme heat, suffocating dust, unusual filth resulting from grease, oil, iron ore and other dirt; working at great heights, in confined spaces and near extremely dangerous machinery. The outcome of these conditions is a spectacular array of abnormal condition payments. In many steel works almost every different job performed by craftsmen on plant maintenance merits an additional payment varying from 3d. to 2s. an hour extra."[2]

[1] NBPI, Report No. 36, *loc. cit.*, p. 62.

[2] Jones and Golding, *op. cit.*, p. 17.

A productivity agreement at the Spencer steel works eliminated payments for abnormal conditions and provided for ex-gratia payments in unforeseen and exceptional circumstances. Abnormal payments, as well as special cost-of-living payments, product bonuses, craftsmen bonuses, and overtime rates have also been consolidated in other productivity agreements, for example Alcan, Fawley, BEA and BOAC and many others.

Clearly, it is possible to preserve the advantages of payment by results—incentive to efficiency and reward for extra effort—while eliminating most of its drawbacks. If both management and workers make an effort, payments systems can be constructed which are fair, stable, objective and inducive to genuine effort and efficiency and which increase worker flexibility. A by-product of this process is often the discovery of new and better ways of doing the job. This in turn leads to revision of productive methods and corresponding changes in work assignments and wage structure.

Systematic and objective work study and job evaluation facilitate valid, rational wage comparisons. Such soundly based comparisons can be extremely valuable to productivity bargainers. They give new validity to the trade union concept of "the rate for the job". They remove serious anomalies in wage structure. And they appeal to the workers' urge for justice and objectivity in wage determination.

Moreover, they need not generate inflation. Like other productivity bargains, they relate to a specific situation and to individual performance within a particular firm. By making "incentives" more genuine, they stimulate output and thereby reduce inflationary pressures. Also they reduce the gap between wage rates and actual earnings, and between time- and piece-worker, and to that extent minimise both wage drift and the process by which drift is transmitted into inflationary leapfrogging.

## Summary

Workers are directly and profoundly affected by industrial changes which alter job content, skill requirements, wage structure and working conditions. Moreover, the complexity and high cost of modern equipment and productive processes make it imperative for management to achieve maximum efficiency in manpower utilisation.

Restrictive work practices—demarcation disputes, overmanning, spurious overtime, work group sanctions and restrictions on entry and on output—constitute a serious obstacle to efficient use of labour. An effective campaign to tackle such practices must be based on understanding of the motives which have given rise to them. These include workers' quest for job and income security, the force of tradition, lax management and the influence of work groups.

Most of the productivity agreements so far concluded have incorporated changes designed to increase efficiency in the utilisation of manpower. These include measures to increase the interchangeability of workers; to reduce the number of men required for particular jobs; to reduce the amount of overtime and provide more flexible working hours; and to reorganise wage structures to make them simpler, more stable, more equitable, more of a stimulus to output and more conducive to flexibility of the work force.

Productivity bargaining has also increased trade union influence over job evaluation and work study. Systematic and objective work study and job evaluation facilitate valid, rational wage comparisons. Such soundly based comparisons can be extremely valuable to productivity bargainers. They give new validity to the trade union concept of "the rate for the job". They remove serious anomalies in wage structure. And they appeal to the workers' urge for justice and objectivity in wage determination.

Moreover, job evaluation and work study need not generate inflation. Like other productivity bargains, they relate to a specific situation and to individual performance within a particular firm. By making "incentives" more genuine, they stimulate output and thereby reduce inflationary pressures. Also they reduce the gap between wage rates and actual earnings, and between time and piece workers, and to that extent minimise both wage drift and the process by which drift is transmitted into inflationary leapfrogging.

## Chapter IV

# Productivity Bargaining and Management

### The Impact on Management of Industrial Change

Industrial change has enormously complicated the management job, particularly in the field of manpower utilisation.

There is a direct and immediate connection between technical equipment and process layout on the one hand and the arrangement of work and work behaviour on the other. Supervisory patterns, job contents, flow and tempo of work, and the quality and temperature of industrial relations in the plant have been shown to bear a close relationship to the technological nature of the work. The appropriate pattern of management will depend on whether the productive process is "unit" or "one-off", large batch, mass production, process, or continuous flow.[1]

Technological developments, the growth in size of factories and companies, more complex and minute divisions of labour—all these have posed new and difficult demands for those responsible for managerial decisions. Decisions must be speedier, more accurate and more coordinated, and at the same time more complex and formal with carefully defined functions and clearcut rules. In the field of personnel management alone, experts have had to be employed for work study and measurement, job evaluation techniques, industrial training, industrial welfare, safety and hygiene and payroll accounting—to mention only a few of the relevant areas.

---

[1] See Joan Woodward, *Industrial Organisation: Theory and Practice*, 1955.

These changes in management hierarchy have in turn affected management employees, no less than production workers, in terms of job content, job security, prestige and salary levels.

Because of the need for expertise and the complex nature of technical management aids like operational research, top level management is, as Galbraith has pointed out, increasingly remote from the centres of decision-making. Indeed it is no longer easy for executives themselves fully to comprehend the basis of decisions that are taken.

One result has been to make management more planning-conscious. There has been a continuing shift from an intuitive, improvised kind of decision-making to a more rational, objective quantified process involving greater precision and consistency at the planning stage of production. In the field of manpower utilisation this has required realistic assessment and negotiation of effort–wage relationships in particular production processes *as a routine part of production planning.*

Rapid changes in job content resulting from new methods and tools of production cause constant changes in job requirements. And because of training lags they create scarcities of particular skills. This makes it essential that management should treat labour as a scarce and valuable resource. Also the high cost of capital equipment requires more flexibility in the utilisation of labour to ensure the most efficient use of expensive equipment.

Thus management is being forced to take a hard look at labour utilisation throughout the plant and to embark on far-reaching changes. These changes have involved work study, job standardisation and evaluation, methods of payment, wage differentials, interchangeability of workers, wider range of duties, more flexibility in hours and an attack on restrictive work practices. They have also necessitated even more division of labour within personnel departments. The NBPI has pointed out that what was only a tiny band of women factory welfare officers in 1914 has by now blossomed into a force of well over 10,000 personnel officers—mostly men.[1]

---

[1] *Donovan Report,* p. 25.

In one sense management is becoming better equipped to cope with the increasing demands upon it. Because of computers it has access to a great deal more accurate and more quickly available information. And it has a wide choice of a bewildering array of new control techniques, for example in the forms of work study, budgetary control, quality control, market research and operational research.

On the other hand there has been a good deal of recent evidence that British management is in danger of losing control over many vital facets of the managerial function. This problem has already been highlighted in Chapter III in connection with restrictive work practices and methods of wage payment. It has led to emergence of what came to be known as "the management gap".[1]

## Productivity Bargaining and the Management Gap

The well-known management consultant, William Allen, one of the architects of the breakthrough productivity agreement as Esso's Fawley refinery, claims that the economy is functioning at half of its potential; that existing capital equipment is being inefficiently used; and that of all the people in a position to do something about the situation, management is most strongly placed and therefore bears the major responsibility for bringing about economic improvements.[2]

The Royal Commission on Trade Unions and Employers' Associations has also been concerned about this problem. It pointed out in the Donovan Report that "studies made and results achieved in this country confirm that there is substantial room for improvement in the efficiency with which labour is used. Management consultants to whom we have talked asserted that industry in this country could, with existing capital, raise its output very considerably."[3]

As evidence of the management gap the Royal Commission cites comparative OECD data submitted to it on increase in levels of

---

[1] A popular term originated by Robert McNamara, now President of the World Bank, in a speech at Jackson, Mississippi on 27 February 1967.

[2] *The Times*, 30 October 1967.

[3] *Donovan Report*, pp. 75–76.

output per person and per man hours for 1955 to 1965 in twelve industrialised countries.

*International Comparisons of Levels of Output per Person*[1] *Employed and of Output per Man Hour in* 1965
Index UK=100

| Country | Adjusted comparative level of real output per person employed in 1965 | Adjusted comparative level of real output per man hour in 1965 |
|---|---|---|
| USA | 184.1 | 188.0 |
| Canada | 137.1 | 140.8 |
| Germany (Federal Republic) | 130.6 | 129.6 |
| Norway | 119.7 | 120.9 |
| Belgium | 118.1 | 119.4 |
| France | 116.0 | 110.7 |
| Netherlands | 114.8 | 106.3 |
| Denmark | 101.8 | 104.2 |
| UK | 100.0 | 100.0 |
| Italy | 87.9 | 88.5 |
| USSR | 82.8 | 89.5 |
| Japan | 74.0 | 74.2 |

The above table highlights the fact that in Western Europe only Italy ranks lower than the United Kingdom on both counts.

The Royal Commission also cites the studies of the Chemical Economic Development Committee which suggests that more men are usually needed to produce the same output in the United Kingdom than in the United States. "It is generally considered . . . that American management is more effective, with objectives more clearly defined, more delegation of responsibility and a simpler managerial structure. American managers are also said to be more cost-conscious where the use of labour is concerned.[2]

---

[1] *Ibid.*, p. 74.
[2] *Ibid.*, p. 75.

The management gap has been confirmed by H. A. Clegg who writes[1] "it is now widely admitted that standards of manpower utilisation are poor throughout much of British industry and services".

Even the Engineering Employers' Federation puts the responsibility on management when it states that[2] "the maintenance of improved standards . . . is a basic inescapable responsibility of management", and cites the following statement by George Cattell (who now heads the new section on industrial relations in the Department for Employment and Productivity): "There is no substitute for planning and administrative foresight or for firm management based upon the exercise of legitimate authority—legitimate because it is derived from superior knowledge and dedication to the purpose of the organisation. Certainly the sanction of lower earnings for lower output is not an effective substitute for management control."

Finally, it is interesting to note that the NBPI in its report on Productivity Agreements[3] stated that "we must point out that responsibility for following the guidelines (for productivity agreements) does not rest equally on the employers and the unions. Both are responsible for seeing that there is a 'direct contribution', that proper controls are included, and for the level of pay. Otherwise the onus rests primarily upon management."

What accounts for the relative inefficiency of British management? There appear to be at least four contributory factors.

1. One is the force of tradition and inertia. There is an acknowledged tendency to take the easy way, not to bother about established practices which have become so familiar that their inefficiency or obsolescence is not even noticed. One of the major employers' groups, the Engineering Employers' Federation, puts first in its list of obstacles to change the lack of management

---

1 *British Industry.*
2 *Loc. cit.*, p. 15.
3 Report No. 36, p. 25.

commitment to change, pointing out that "it is clear that the innate conservatism of organisation is a particularly patent obstacle. New methods require the disturbing of established routines, require increased thought, patience and effort from managers, require in short a commitment to change."[1]

2. Another factor has been a "cost-plus" mentality that attaches low priority to cutting costs. This attitude stems from a confidence that high costs can be easily passed on to consumers in the form of higher prices. This confidence in turn is fostered by full employment, by inflation and by the monopolistic discretion afforded by size, price leadership and a "cosy" business atmosphere in which management condones or even connives at restrictive practices on the part both of businessmen and of workers.

The NBPI has found that managements are often so concerned with increasing output and meeting demand that they give little thought to problems of rising costs and long-term competitiveness of enterprises. "If it is more important to meet the order book than to keep down production costs, management control over payment systems is inclined to slacken. Again, where the need to recruit and retain workers overrides other objectives, management tends to become more concerned that the system should produce earnings which are attractive than that increased earnings should be matched by a high performance from the worker."[2]

3. In part, however, management laxness in the field of manpower utilisation is simply a consequence of the fact that managers don't know what their wage costs are. Many firms do not equip themselves with even elementary cost data. According to H. A. Clegg, "Boards of directors don't—or won't—know what is possible. And all too often they don't know the facts. They don't know in detail the wage structures in their own firm, grade by grade. They don't know about overtime—how much is being worked systematically, week after week, sometimes for years on

---

[1] Engineering Employers Federation; *loc. cit.*, p. 13.
[2] Report No. 65, p. 18.

end. And they don't realise the potential of productivity bargaining."[1]

And the Confederation of British Industry, in a document containing an action programme to improve the nation's industrial performance, stated[2] that there is some evidence that "alert and technically qualified middle management are not always able to make full use of their abilities because those above them are not always fully aware of new techniques".

4. But perhaps the main cause is management's reluctance to resist the pressure of work groups on the shop floor. Manpower questions are often left to the personnel department which is more concerned to avoid trouble than to improve the use of resources. The easier path is to pay heavily for overtime in order to attract workers; to permit overmanning to avoid redundancies, redeployment, retraining and reorganisation of work practices; and to accept go-slows, loose rates and lax timekeeping to avoid friction. In many cases it is likely that management has overestimated the force of worker attachment to restrictive work practices and hence the cost of "buying them out".

"Management averts its eyes and work group control systems grow unchecked without ever being called upon to relate themselves to a rational, consistent managerial policy. Management thus preserves the pretence of maintaining its prerogatives but nevertheless connives at the extension of unilateral regulation by work groups. Precisely because this extension of informal work-group regulation is not met by management, it represents a genuine loss of managerial control."[3]

Since so many fingers have been pointed so directly at management, it is encouraging to report that the NBPI found in its exhaustive study on Productivity Agreements that productivity bargaining has made for striking progress in the struggle to narrow

---

[1] *Financial Times,* June 30 1967.

[2] *Industrial Management and the Next Two Years,* published 26 February 1968.

[3] Fox, *op. cit.,* p. 14.

the management gap. This evidence is worth quoting in some detail:

> Except at Milford Haven (where the agreement we have studied came after a series of productivity agreements) and in ICI (where the agreement has not yet been applied) all the managements included in the reference have been radically affected by the experience of their productivity agreements. Planning the agreements already had an effect by inducing cost-consciousness, by providing new information about performance and new methods of assessing performance, and by directing attention to the possibility of changing methods of work. . . .
>
> The length and scope of the negotiations at all levels brought their negotiators into closer touch with the unions than before; and because far more managers were brought into the process than in conventional negotiations, many of them were made closely aware for the first time of the consequences for industrial relations of technical and financial decisions. . . . The experience of applying the agreements, together with their provisions on overtime, flexibility, manning and so on has brought about *nothing less than a revolution in managerial control over working hours and practices in many of the undertakings affected.*
>
> In addition there have been changes in organisation, in personnel and the provision of training. Generally speaking, therefore, management is better informed and better organised than before the agreements.[1] (Italics added.)

## Productivity Bargaining as a Challenge to Management

A productivity agreement is not an easy road to industrial peace and increased output at lower unit costs. Nor, as Flanders pointed out, is it necessarily "conducive to the quiet life".

The bargaining that precedes the achievement of an agreement is a long, complex and arduous process that tends to generate what the Engineering Employers' Federation has termed "negotiating fatigue". And the successful implementation of the agreement, once it has been accepted, is never-ending. It involves constant and alert supervision, continuing consultation with workers, and machinery for dealing with grievances which experience has shown are likely to be more frequent, not less.

More specifically, productivity bargaining imposes on management a number of taxing demands.

---

[1] Report No. 36, p. 25.

1. It requires careful assessment of costs and benefits, and detailed planning for implementing agreed changes. This involves making sure that layout, scheduling and reporting of work progress are such as to provide a steady flow of work. And it means far-sighted *manpower scheduling* for purposes of redeploying workers, planning retraining programmes and taking early steps to avoid redundancies.

For most firms such planning-consciousness will be more of an innovation than an extension of normal managerial activities. In a survey of 300 selected large and medium firms in the metal industry, the Manpower Research Unit of what is now the Department of Employment and Productivity found that less than one in four makes forecasts beyond two years ahead, and half do none at all. Only one in forty makes forecasts for all types of employees.

But it is likely that those managements which are serious about their planning efforts will increasingly find it possible to obtain assistance and information from their employer associations, from the Little Neddies for their industrial sectors, and from the Manpower Research Unit.

2. Productivity bargaining also usually calls for a restructuring of the management hierarchy itself. This relates particularly to a strengthening of the authority, resources and responsibilities of personnel departments. So far the personnel function has seldom been on an equal footing with financial, production or marketing functions. Productivity bargaining, however, requires that personnel officers must not be isolated within the firm. The personnel department must maintain close relationships with all other levels of enterprise. And it must be integrated into the decision-making process. Also personnel officers will have to be equipped with information on manpower needs; specialist staff capable of obtaining and using the information; and authority and resources for handling recruitment, redeployment, training, negotiation and consultation programmes.

3. The support and cooperation of supervisory staff is essential. And they will need to be thoroughly trained for their new

responsibilities. Foremen play a key role in the implementation of a productivity agreement. It is their job to allocate jobs, schedule overtime, handle workshop disputes in the first instance, control PBR systems and so on. Thus it is the foreman who must be taught to worry about costs as well as output.

> In the past supervisors were involved in a good deal of pretence. They were supposed to be in control of overtime and of the pace of work, but practices tolerated by management prevented their control being effective, and protected them from criticism. Now (after introduction of productivity bargaining) they are directly responsible for seeing that improved performance is achieved and cannot plead the old excuses. The application of the agreements therefore made it possible for them to do their jobs more effectively, but also made heavy demands on them.[1]

4. Management will also have to be constantly aware of, and take into account, the attitudes of work groups within the plant. As Fox has indicated "it is scarcely possible to conceive of such (productivity bargaining) ventures standing any chance of continuing success except where managers maintain a constant intuitive awareness, *grounded in intellectual understanding*, of the diversity of group interests, objectives and motivations." (Italics added.)[2]

5. Agreement on a productivity bargain comes only at the end of a long, persistent, gruelling process of discussion with unions and with workers at plant level. There is increasing recognition by management of the need for open, patient discussion—a joint problem-solving approach—in order to modify deep-seated beliefs, fears and norms of behaviour, and to reassure workers as to the future.

The well-publicised difficulties of ICI with its Manpower Utilisation and Payments Structure agreements have underlined the crucial importance of good communications throughout the negotiating process. At two of the biggest sites—Wilton and Billingham on Teeside—the deal ran into immediate trouble. At Wilton the unions never got round the negotiating table; at Billingham positive

---

[1] NBPI, Report No. 36, p. 25.
[2] Fox, *op. cit.*, p. 10.

manning proposals were agreed and then rejected by a mass meeting of AEU workers.[1]

Plant officials are now agreed that there should have been much more preliminary preparation and communication with the workers. The signing of the agreement and the announcement that Wilton and Billingham were to be trial sites had been made on the same day. Learning from experience, a subsequent and successful introduction of the agreement at Gloucester was preceded by several months of induction to prepare the necessary changes in attitude and to permit suggestions on ways of improving production. Job descriptions were drawn up after extensive investigation by union and management working parties with shop floor workers kept constantly informed and often preparing the changes themselves.[2]

A large part of the Engineering Employers' Federation brochure on Productivity Bargaining is devoted to the importance of communications—within management and supervisory ranks, between management and trade union officials, between union officials and their members, and between management and employees. The Federation emphasises the setting up of "a communication link between management and the shop floor, to let it be seen that there would be nothing secret in the way the job was done, to give the men as well as their official representatives the opportunity to ventilate problems and the consultant the chance to discuss work done, give out information about plans, and so on".[3]

There has been much discussion as to the appropriate stage at which to bring trade union representatives into the negotiation process. In some cases they have been presented with a fully worked-out set of proposals (three Esso agreements, Alcan). In others, they have been brought in earlier for a common management–union approach (British Oxygen, Mobil Oil). And in some cases the approach has been in-between, that is, joint discussions of the

---

[1] British Industry Week, 19 January 1968.
[2] *Financial Times*, 26 January 1968.
[3] Engineering Employers' Federation, *loc. cit.*, pp. 19–20.

separate components of proposals, but formulation of the final package of proposals by management alone (ICI, Electricity Supply).

At the implementation stage, too, it is essential to give out information regularly on the progress of the agreement. The Engineering Employers' Federation recommends the device of monthly bulletins to give details of output, production, comparisons of productivity to that of competitors, etc. It also suggests that attitude surveys on the shop floor can be informative to management and help to create a more favourable atmosphere.

6. Finally, many managements which embark on productivity bargaining are confronted with the problem of working out their relationship with the employers' association to which they are affiliated.

Several major productivity agreements have been concluded by companies which were not federated to employers' associations. These include Esso, Mobil, Shell and British Petroleum because there is no employers' association which conducts negotiations covering oil refining; similarly the gases division of British Oxygen is not covered by membership of an association. ICI has an exceptional arrangement with the Chemical Industries Association permitting it to conduct its own negotiations with the unions.

On the other hand, several companies had to withdraw from employer associations in order to conclude productivity deals—including Esso Distribution and Milford Haven, Mobil and Alcan. And in the shipping industry Esso and Shell have had difficulties with the Shipping Federation, but these seem to be on the way to solution.[1] In general there is a consensus of opinion in management circles as well as within the Government that employers' associations have an important and useful supporting role to play in productivity bargaining.

The Confederation of British Industry has endorsed the principle of productivity bargaining and advocates integration of national and local machinery for productivity bargaining.

---

[1] *Donovan Report,* p. 198.

> It is envisaged that guidelines for the negotiation of productivity agreements, suitably adapted to the needs of individual industries, might be laid down in national agreements, as has already been done in the Chemical Industry, it being left to employers and trade union representatives to negotiate detailed agreements at plant level within the scope provided by the principles of the guidelines. In this way the industry-wide agreement would constitute a framework for the development and coordination of productivity bargaining at plant level.[1]

The NBPI recommends[2] that the best course for an association to follow would be to issue guidelines suitably modified to suit the industry's own circumstances. Members would be expected to observe these in any productivity agreements they might sign, and would otherwise observe the existing agreements. The association would follow negotiations closely, register the resulting agreements, and circulate information to other members. One or two associations are already making progress along these lines; others it suggests, should follow suit.

The Engineering Employers' Federation has pointed out[3] that the compiling of definitive guidelines in an industry of the size and complexity of engineering would present many difficulties. It suggests, however, that the Federation could appoint additional National Technical Committees on a trade sectional basis to cope with the task of designing meaningful industry guidelines. In addition, local associations could directly help member firms through consultation on objectives of productivity bargaining, assistance in drawing up agreements, registering them and following them up, and circulating members with information on the progress of the agreements.

Finally, the Royal Commission suggest[4] that many large companies still feel so committed to their associations that the reforms introduced by productivity agreements can be carried out within a reasonable period only if supported by those associations. Moreover, many smaller companies which are not yet equipped to

---

[1] Confederation of British Industry, *loc. cit.*, p. 13.
[2] Report No. 36, p. 36.
[3] Engineering Employers' Federation, *loc. cit.*, p. 17.
[4] *Donovan Report, loc. cit.*, p. 43.

negotiate their own agreements with the unions will want to rely on negotiating through their associations for some time to come.

## Summary

Industrial change has imposed difficult demands on management which bears the onus for increasing productivity; and at the same time has profoundly affected job content, security, prestige and incomes of management staff. Although management is better equipped than ever before with relevant information and control techniques, there is growing evidence of a "management gap" which has seriously impaired the competitiveness of British exports. This gap appears to be a compound of tradition and inertia, "cost-plus" mentality, inadequate cost analysis and vacillation of management in the face of pressure by work groups.

Productivity bargaining has enormous potential for helping management to meet the challenge of industrial change. It can provide new information, induce cost-consciousness, facilitate necessary changes in organisation and work practices and in training, and bring management into closer touch with workers.

But productivity bargaining is not easy. It entails a long, arduous process of negotiation and implementation through careful supervision and continuing consultation. It also calls for planning and coordination; restructuring of the management hierarchy; support and training for supervisory staff; sensitivity to attitudes of work groups; effective communication within management ranks, between management and trade union officials, between trade unions and their members, and between management and employees; and resolution of tensions between firms and the employers' associations to which they are affiliated.

## Chapter V

# Productivity Bargaining and Worker Security

### Threats to Workers from Industrial Change

Changes in techniques and equipment, work practices and job content are a threat to traditional job demarcations, customary skills, worker autonomy over jobs, incomes, career continuity and status, work groups, job satisfaction and job security.

The very prospect of change, in whatever direction, is unsettling and disruptive to workers. The content of the job may be altered in a way that diminishes satisfaction in the work. It may require different work methods and skills, loss of investment in training, and the need to retrain in order to cope with the new requirements. Or it may mean downgrading and consequent changes in status and in pay.

Change may also entail disruption of closely-knit work groups. And workers' control over their jobs is likely to decline as the production process is increasingly regulated and determined at higher levels by technicians. The more complicated and integrated the process of decision-making in the firm becomes, the greater will be the tendency to make the workers mere instruments and subordinates rather than active participants in the process of economic growth. Experience becomes less important than explicit instruction, and work initiative is restricted.

In many important respects *working conditions have improved.* The physical environment in the workshop is safer, more hygienic and more attractive. Machines have taken over the less pleasant, more strenuous repetitive routine tasks. The rapid development of ergonomics—the science of human engineering which combines techniques like work study and design engineering with the findings of physiology, anatomy and experimental psychology—is steadily reducing physical and nervous strain and fatigue.

Many workers now have greater physical mobility on the job and more transferability as between jobs, a grasp of several related processes, and a better understanding of the whole process. There is increased opportunity in many cases for exercise of judgement, resourcefulness and responsibility, and more frequent contact with technical staff. And there may be more scope for development of a sense of solidarity with emphasis on membership in a team responsible for maintaining a group norm rather than on individual efforts to exceed a specified limit.

On the other hand, for some workers there are *serious drawbacks in the modern workshop setting*. Many derive less, rather than more, satisfaction from their work because of loss of a sense of participation and achievement as the work process is broken down into a series of elementary operations requiring limited skill.

There are many factors which increase nervous strain and mental fatigue. These include greater noise, faster tempo, lack of control over pace of work, the necessity for constant alertness and close concentration, and the heavy burden of responsibility imposed by awareness of the serious consequences of an error.

Boredom is often induced by the monotony of the operation, the infrequency of interruptions and the isolation and reduced opportunity for social intercourse. Finally, there is a considerable increase in shift work and night work (motivated by the high cost of capital equipment and the importance of avoiding shutdowns). These have obvious drawbacks in terms of family life, social and recreational activities and disturbance of bodily rhythm.

Most frightening of all, technological change carries with it the growing threat of redundancy. It may mean loss of jobs and withering away of alternative job opportunities. It also involves "silent firings" or closed doors for new entrants to the labour force. Automation threatens not only the worker's particular job, but also his skill—the way of earning a living that he has acquired so laboriously over the years.

It is more than his livelihood that is at stake. For many workers technological change is likely to mean loss of status. When a particular skill becomes obsolete so do the worker's prestige, his standing with his colleagues, perhaps even his pride in the work and some of the privileges associated with the craft in terms of notice, holidays, sick pay, redundancy pay, opportunities for overtime and independence of supervision.

A technological change means both a change in what the worker *does* in the firm and a change in what he *is* in relation to the firm, the various groups inside, the social groups outside and the community as a whole.

## The Need for Worker Assent to Change

Earlier chapters have indicated the deeply-felt need for far-reaching changes designed to increase efficiency in utilisation of manpower. It is equally clear—and to this management agrees—that the primary responsibility and initiative for bringing about these changes rests with management.

But this still leaves open the question of why the answer lies in productivity bargaining between the two sides of industry. *Why does not management take the necessary action through unilateral decision*?

The answer is that workers will thwart those management decisions which they believe to threaten their security. The impact of technological change is such that management must woo the worker and "buy" his cooperation. In enormous plants where the jobs and status of dozens or hundreds or thousands of workers are at stake, it is not possible for an employer to introduce and implement new methods without their acquiescence. It is true that many technical and other changes are continually being introduced by management quite easily without challenge of any kind. But where workers feel unjustly treated they will not cooperate. And we have seen that work groups have effective means of obstruction. Hence management must seek their support and understanding by keeping them informed, discussing with them, and giving them a voice in planning and decision-making. Above all, workers must be compensated for any consequent losses in income, status or security. Productivity bargaining is bargaining to make changes acceptable.

Now more than ever before workers, by their attitudes and actions, can determine the speed at which change takes place and the extent to which its promise is realised. The consent of the governed, which is a widely recognised principle of political life, is rapidly penetrating the field of industrial relations in all major industrialised countries.

The need for consent of the workers to the kind of changes involved in productivity agreements was dramatically illustrated by the difficulties, already cited, which ICI experienced with its major plants on Tees-side involving some 21,000 shop employees. Many of these workers, particularly those associated with the Amalgamated Union of Engineering and Foundry Workers, were jealous of their craft status which was threatened by a blurring of demarcation lines between craft and process workers. Hence the Manpower Utilisation and Payments Structure scheme could not be forced through by ICI. Although the scheme involved a substantial pay increase, it became clear that for it to succeed there would have to be a good deal of persuasion and discussion to whittle down the opposition. The craft workers' reaction was reported to be: "The money is not good enough. ICI exploded all this in people's faces and they are still recoiling as from a squib."[1]

It is also clear that productivity bargains cannot be forced through against worker opposition simply on the basis of the argument that they are "in the national interest". As the TUC pointed out:

> There can be no national interest divorced from individual interests. People in employment comprise a large part of the nation. . . . No one would deny in the abstract that progress involves change and that changing jobs is an important element in this change. Yet if the change produces a benefit for the nation as a whole trade unions ask why it should involve a loss to those directly involved. . . .
>
> While trade unionists have a considerable stake in economic growth, they will continue to scrutinise changes which are proposed to ensure that these developments . . . do in fact bring benefits to those directly affected which are greater than the costs involved.[2]

---

[1] *Financial Times,* 26 January 1968.
[2] TUC, *op. cit.,* pp. 35–6.

Indeed, the TUC is increasingly concerned over the threat to workers from industrial change, especially when it takes the form of company mergers. In a more recent report[1] it stated:

> Unless this accelerated process of change in the company sector is intelligently and responsibly handled it must increase the insecurity of many groups of workers. Yet the measure of control and intervention that has been developed so far provides no protection for the interests of wage and salary earners whose jobs and prospects may be suddenly and violently affected. The consumer has a measure of protection through the Monopolies Act. Shareholders are receiving the protection of a revised code of conduct for takeovers instituted by the Stock Exchange Council. The IRC seeks to further the public interest over correct economic and technological choices. None of these agencies considers workers' interests as such. There is no code of conduct accepted by the managements of the firms concerned to ensure that the human needs of the workers are adequately safeguarded. Statutory protection is only marginal as yet.

Recently there has been a discussion within the Government concerning just such a code of conduct for protection of workers' interests in the event of mergers, and a White Paper on the subject is expected. The TUC would like such a code to cover the need for full recognition of unions; provision of information to unions and members; procedures for the systematic examination and harmonisation of wages and conditions and industrial relations' practices within the new company; and special procedures for major closures, involving appropriate manpower planning and stronger provisions for compensation not only for redundancy but also *for downgrading.*

## Productivity Bargaining and Earnings

1. *Level of Earnings*

Invariably a productivity bargain increases the level of pay, sometimes dramatically. The bulk of these increases have been in return for savings in manpower or for reduction of overtime. However, a few workers have had to forfeit large overtime earnings and may have suffered actual losses in take-home pay. Usually, however, new levels of pay are based on the principle that all of the

---

[1] *Economic Review,* 1968, *loc. cit.,* p. 18.

workers directly involved, and sometimes these less directly involved, should gain something in terms of earnings.

Moreover, pay increases are usually granted at the outset without waiting for the changes in productivity to work themselves through. The workers are, as it were, paid on account once they have agreed to changes in working practices. This approach is accepted by most employers, and it is definitely favoured by the TUC:

> A productivity bargain done on the cheap is not likely to produce worthwhile results. If it is to result in genuine increases in production by facilitating radical changes in manning or other work practices it is going to cost money, and it is not realistic to assume that there should be no increases in pay until the full returns of productivity have been achieved. In the short run therefore the negotiation of productivity agreements may even pose problems in terms of incomes policy before they become fully self-financing, but it is nevertheless important that there should be room for the development of those new techniques within the context of an overall policy.[1]

The NBPI finds that there is no clear overall guide to the size of pay increases to be negotiated under productivity bargaining:

> The increase in pay which can be achieved in a productivity agreement is indeterminate and open to bargaining. It should be sufficient to elicit the required changes, but should normally provide a contribution to price stability; and it must be possible to bargain for radical changes in methods against a higher reward. The judgment must be made on the facts in each case. To lay down a rigid rule of one-third to the worker, one-third to the employer and one-third to the consumer would kill many valuable agreements from the start and permit the exploitation of the consumer in other cases.[2]

### 2. *Stability of Earnings*

Experience has proved, however, that workers are as much concerned about stability of earnings as about their level. Hence the importance which they attach to changes introduced in the course of productivity bargaining which have had the effect of stabilising the amount of take-home pay from week to week.

The most significant of these changes has been to consolidate extras into basic rates. These extras include incentive bonuses and

---

[1] Economic Review, *loc. cit.*, p. 25.
[2] NBPI Report No. 36, *op. cit.*, p. 39.

other special payments. The other major influence has been the steps taken to reduce differences between white-collar and manual workers with respect to their wage packets. This has involved putting manual workers on annual wages or salaries which are paid weekly instead of hourly rates. It has also meant allowing them short periods without loss of pay for approved absences. And it has put them on the same basis as white-collar workers with respect to sick pay, pensions and holiday payments. More stable earnings in turn make it easier for workers to obtain house mortgages and hire purchase arrangements.

Issues of status and security have been crucial in working out productivity agreements with seamen employed on tankers of oil distribution companies. Esso, for example, has developed a new Marine Personnel Policy under which the tanker fleet will be manned by permanent crews who will be salaried employees of the company with the status and privileges of their colleagues in other departments, and opportunities for further training and promotion.

## Productivity Bargaining and Job Security

Productivity bargains are designed to improve manpower utilisation. This means that the objective is to do the job with fewer workers. To management this means manpower savings. But to workers it means redundancies. Hence they are reluctant to become parties to such agreements unless there are built-in safeguards, carefully spelled out, with respect to their particular jobs.

So far the majority of productivity agreements have been concluded in expanding industries, with the notable exception of railways and bus services. Hence the redundancy issue has not been highlighted. Nevertheless there has been enough experience to indicate some of the methods that can be employed to allay fears concerning job security.

One is natural wastage, or the process of letting the workforce reduce itself through death and retirements and filling the vacancies through redeployment within the plant rather than through recruitment. This process is occurring all the time in many companies without being incorporated into formal collective agreements.

But it becomes a reliable method only where there is formal planning which makes it possible to forecast reductions sufficiently in advance; hence its suitability for productivity agreements. In some productivity agreements the natural wastage approach has been even more explicit. Examples are Fawley, Alcan, BEA, Petrochemicals and Mobil Oil where reliance on natural wastage was made the basis for a "no-redundancy" guarantee. But as the NBPI has pointed out, such guarantees "test the accuracy of manpower forecasting".

The natural wastage approach is sometimes fortified by an element of persuasion through offering inducements to *early retirement*. This is a device that is being widely experimented with in the United States and on the Continent.

At Fawley, improvements in manpower planning were introduced after the initial agreement proved to be inadequate. This Voluntary Separation Scheme was the precursor of similar arrangements in its distribution sector.

> During 1964 Management drew up detailed plans of the numbers of men surplus to requirements. The trade unions were consulted and they informally agreed to permit the departure of men under a scheme of 'voluntary separation'. In October the existing staff early retirement scheme was extended to all employees; men not eligible who left were to be paid a sum of money calculated on the basis of age and length of service. Esso had intended that manpower reduction should only be on the M. & C. side, but was unwilling to refuse process workers who wanted to go and, in any case, was not averse to seeing their average age lowered. Thus of some 400 men who volunteered to leave, 80 were from the process department. Nearly all the rest were semi-skilled men. Esso went to great trouble to get employment for those who left and were helped in this by the Ministry of Labour. Some of the men were sent to Government retraining centres. At the end of the scheme all those concerned who wanted further employment had been placed in new jobs.[1]

Because of the experience at Fawley, Esso were more cautious in their productivity agreements for Milford Haven. Instead of a "no-redundancy" pledge it incorporated a general "statement of intention" which was actually quite specific in its provisions.

---

[1] NBPI Report No. 36, *loc. cit.*, p. 50.

> We do not envisage that the implementation of this agreement would give rise to anyone being made redundant. However, should any redundancy arise we believe that the necessary reduction in manpower would, in the first instance, be covered by natural wastage. If this were not so the company would be prepared to assist in placing any redundant personnel and would be prepared, if necessary, to give active consideration to re-training anyone redundant, so that he would be equipped to find alternative employment. We should also be prepared to give anyone affected at least three months' notice of redundancy, the last month of which would count as the month's notice required under the Contracts of Employment Act, 1963. We should also be prepared in this situation to make severance payments at a more favourable rate than is called for under the proposed Redundancy Payments Bill.[1]

## Redundancy Legislation

In Britain it is now widely accepted that State intervention is essential to ensure workers against the adverse affects of loss of job.

The various motives which have led to this conclusion correspond with varying interpretations of the justification for redundancy benefits. Some think of severance pay as compensation for loss of employment; or even as a supplement to unemployment benefits. Others see it as a cash benefit to enable workers to meet financial obligations; or recognition of past services; or compensation for loss of promotion prospects or property rights in the job; or additional but postponed wage payment. And some are primarily interested in the influence which the cost of redundancy benefits can have in inhibiting employers from dismissing workers.

Whatever the interpretation, there are few who question the need for redundancy legislation. And there are many who are demanding increases in benefits under that legislation.

Some of the legislation passed in the last five years has aimed at lessening the hardships of redundancy. Men can no longer be fired on the spot. Under the Contracts of Employment Act of 1963, most people have the right to a minimum period of notice of termination of employment varying from one week for an employee who has been with a firm for up to six months, to four

---

[1] Jones and Golding, *op. cit.*, pp. 19–20.

weeks for a person who has been with his employer for five years or more.

The financial blow of redundancy has also been eased. The Redundancy Payments Act ensures financial compensation for all workers made redundant (provided they have been with their employer for at least two years). In certain circumstances it can also apply to people who are laid off or put on short time for extended periods. Payments are made on a scale which is based on age and length of service. In theory employers bear the total cost of redundancy payments. All employers make a contribution to the Redundancy Fund of one shilling per week for each man on their payroll and sixpence for each woman. If they make redundancy payments to their workers, they can then reclaim from the Fund most of the money they have had to pay out.

Recent mergers and the redundancy they have caused have spotlighted the need to impose some conditions on employers who plan redundancies. The Government has begun consultations about a redundancy code for employers.

> Hiring and firing is still, in Britain, an employer's prerogative. In France and Germany an employer who intends to make workers redundant must consult the workers' representatives in the firm. But British employers have no such obligations under the law. Firms' attitudes vary enormously. In most firms the practice of consulting unions on plans for rationalisation at an early stage is well established. But there are exceptions. The blame for this tends to lie on both sides. Some unions, particularly in engineering, have shown a marked reluctance to face the problem of redundancy, and still refuse to discuss it. And some managements fear that open discussions will cause the unions to revolt. Or they fear that the firm will lose men in a rush and so be unable to run down production gradually.[1]

It is likely that pressures will mount for improvements in redundancy legislation. The National Executive of the Labour Party, for example, has stated that:

> There is a need to increase the protection afforded to workers, to shield them from the consequence of mergers and rationalisation, going far beyond the right to compensation for redundancy under the Redundancy Payments Act. This might be met by a Redundancy Procedures Act to ensure for all workers the best standards of industrial

---

[1] *Economist,* 13 April 1968.

behaviour won by union bargaining or adopted by progressive managements.

The Board of Trade should in any case use the powers of scrutiny it possesses under the Monopolies and Mergers Act to ensure adequate warning, consultation and that provision is made for any workers who may be affected by such mergers; and the relevant unions must be consulted whenever merger proposals involving the I.R.C. are under discussion.[1]

Government legislation can also help redundant workers by assisting them in finding new jobs. The public employment exchange is not widely enough used, but efforts are being made to improve it in terms of siting, appearance, amenities, staffing, administration and providing teams of guidance officers for adults. The possibility of use of computers for circulating vacancies and matching them with applications is being considered.

Geographical mobility of workers is increased by a number of financial aids including the Resettlement Transfer Scheme, the Key Workers' Scheme and Nucleus Labour Force Scheme. All of these feature fares to new areas or training establishments, settling-in allowances, lodging allowances, fares for visits home, subsidies for bringing families to new areas and for moving furniture, and grants for incidental expenses and those incurred in buying and selling homes.

The alternative approach is to attempt to bring jobs to workers in areas of above average unemployment. This has been the purpose of legislation on regional development such as the Local Employment Act of 1960, the Industrial Development Act of 1966 and regional differentials under the Selective Employment Tax.

The Government also helps redundant workers through its training centres. As of April 1968 there were 38 such training centres, with 8,000 places and capacity for training 13,500 a year. It is planned to increase the number to 55 by 1970 to a capacity of training 23,000 a year.

Most of the training courses last for six months, often with an additional period of training in industry. For people who attend the centres the outlook is good; about 90 per cent get jobs as soon as they leave.

---

[1] *Industrial Democracy,* statement presented to the Labour Party by its National Executive Committee at the Annual Conference in October 1968.

> There are, though, difficulties. Some union officials object to a job going to a man who has spent a mere six months in a government training centre when other applicants may have spent five years as apprentices. And though the unions at national level cooperate in the acceptance of men trained at government centres there are long-standing local difficulties about the acceptance of trainees in certain parts of Scotland, in Manchester and on Tyneside.[1]

Clearly the major responsibility for retraining workers must rest on private industry. Many private employers use senior staff as instructors, employ instructors in schools run for their employees, or combine in-plant instruction with day release or occasional courses at technical colleges or similar establishments. Too often, however, they look upon retraining as the responsibility of the Government.

Under the Industrial Training Act of 1964 employers are required to finance the activities of the training boards by paying a levy related to the size of their payrolls, which they will be able to reclaim in allowances upon proof that they have carried out satisfactory training schemes. There is no doubt that the boards have made a lot of headway in stimulating training in industry.

> By approving modular training systems they have shortened training courses and led to the improvement of some apprenticeship systems—systems which have been the major bugbear in improving the efficiency of training methods. Over the three years from 1964 to 1967, there was an increase of 15 per cent in the number of people under training in manufacturing industry. The total number of people receiving training in industry is now estimated to be well over 30,000.[2]

The entire system of training within industry is being reorganised, rationalised and subjected to the jurisdiction of a training board for each major industry. It is intended that the level of training shall be improved and brought to a comparable standard of excellence in all establishments. The levy will force firms doing little or no training to contribute to the costs of the others from whom they have, in the past, sometimes "poached" trained workers.

---

[1] *Economist,* 13 April 1968.
[2] *Economist,* 13 April 1968.

**Summary**

Industrial change constitutes a threat to traditional job demarcations, customary skills, worker autonomy over jobs, incomes, career continuity and status, work groups, job satisfaction and job security. Technological change affects what the worker *does* in the firm and what he *is* relative to the firm, the various groups inside it, the social groups outside and the community as a whole.

Because industrial change represents a threat to workers, employers can obtain their consent to change only if their fears can be allayed. When workers feel endangered or unjustly treated, they will not cooperate. Trade unions and work groups dispose of effective means for obstructing production.

Productivity bargaining is bargaining to make change acceptable to workers. It does this by increasing the level and the stability of earnings and by enhancing job security through provisions for training, for promotion, for avoiding redundancy through natural wastage and early retirement, and for compensating for redundancy where it is inevitable. The effectiveness of productivity bargaining from the point of view of worker security is greatly increased by redundancy legislation, including the Contracts of Employment Act, the Redundancy Payments Act, the public employment services and the Industrial Training Act.

## Chapter VI

# Productivity Bargaining and Fair Shares

### Productivity Bargaining and Wage Differentials

*The "Solidarity" Concept*

In theory trade unionists have long been wedded to the concept of "the rate for the job".

By this they do not mean the elimination of wage differentials. Workers, they feel, should be adequately rewarded for genuine differences in effort, in skill, in responsibility and in working conditions. The objective is rather "equal pay for equal work".

But this in turn implies a rational, orderly, consistent wage structure right across industry. Workers on equivalent jobs should earn "the standard rate" regardless of the sector of industry or the particular employer.

In short, it is felt that differentials should be determined by *the nature of the work* and not by profitability, efficiency, commercial circumstances or negotiating strength of the individual employer or worker.

The TUC has stated that trade union stress on solidarity reflects concern over inequality of distribution not only in ownership of capital but also with respect to employment income. "Agreement on the need for redistribution in this field implies that some people would be willing to forego part of what they could earn to assist those in a weaker position . . . it would be mistaken to think that phrases such as brotherhood and social justice are only rhetoric. Trade unionists have a strong sense of community and it would be wrong to assume that any apparently disinterested act can only be explained in terms of long-term self interest."[1]

---

[1] TUC, *Evidence to the Royal Commission on Trade Unions and Employers' Association*, p. 37, 1966.

*The Actual Wage Structure*

In practice, however, the wage structure has never even approximated the solidarity ideal. It was never deliberately and scientifically planned to conform to an orderly pattern of comparative job contents. Wage differentials are haphazard and chaotic. The "rate for the job" has always been theoretical only, and perhaps it always will be.

This is because wages and the relation they bear to each other are not planned. Wage decisions are *ad hoc* and opportunistic. They just happen for all sorts of historical and accidental reasons which bear little relation to skill and effort, or even to market supply and demand.

Predominant among these reasons are tradition and custom. Also there is the fact that "status" or "prestige" jobs tend to command salaries quite out of line with the arduousness or responsibility of even the special skills required for the work; and so do the more pleasant and interesting jobs. Another significant factor has been the bargaining strength and skill of vested interests, often narrow craft interests.

Also in the tight labour market of the last decade or so, the addition to national rates of local incentive bonuses of all kinds has greatly added to the confusion. Incentive earnings constantly increase in response to labour market pressures and technological changes. But these increases are very unevenly distributed—and again, they bear little relation to any principles of rational wage structure. The pattern of incomes depends rather on the bargaining skill of the groups involved, sectional rates of productivity growth, institutional differences, the length of production runs, and the impact of technical change on particular job contents.

Moreover, time workers do not benefit from this local bargaining unless they happen to be subject to 'lieu" rates. Many semi-skilled workers on PBR—and even some unskilled workers—earn more than the highest paid skilled time workers. And some semi-skilled PBR workers earn more than skilled PBR workers.

In view of the inequities and anomalies resulting from such an haphazard process, there is no objective basis for discussion of wage differentials. But the problem of differentials has become a major cause of unrest and dissatisfaction on both sides of industry —and an increasing source of worry to the Government.

Anomalies in wage structure frustrate the solidarity objective of trade unionists, and they create competitive difficulties for individual employers. They also cause overall economic difficulties by generating secondary earnings drift and the "comparability" process of leapfrogging which is a major source of inflation.

The more disorderly the wage structure becomes, the more the trade unions feel impelled to strive for solidarity in order to protect the interests of lower-paid workers. But they are far from clear as to how this should be achieved.

Their confusion stems basically from the fact that they are pulled in several directions simultaneously. They want preferential treatment for the lower-paid in the interest of more equal income distribution. They want to correct anomalies in the wage structure. They want to reward increases in productivity. There are many among them—especially in the higher wage brackets—who are opposed to drastic narrowing of differentials. And they are publicly committed, through the TUC, to support the incomes policy and not to allow any of these other objectives to degenerate into a "comparability" scramble.

*For example:* in the *1968 Economic Review* the TUC states that the General Council have been working on the assumption that an anomaly exists where an employer pays significantly lower rates for work from which another, or possibly the same, employer is paying a much higher rate. *But* "this definition is not itself entirely satisfactory since extended too far it simply becomes an argument in favour of comparability. For this reason the General Council have applied this criterion very selectively, and in the main only in low-paid non-manual areas, and they recognise that any precise application would involve them in trying to answer the unanswerable question of what a 'just' wage is for a specified category of work."

*Or* "There may be a few instances in which it is not in the national interest that a specific group of workers should be paid substantially less than comparable groups (the Civil Service is a case in point), but in general the General Council intend to treat rigorously arguments about anomalies and comparability."[1]

The TUC has sought for more "solidarity" by trying to ensure that while all wage earners get some increases, the lower-paid get proportionately more. *But* it has experienced difficulties in carrying out this policy. "Faced with recommendations by the Incomes Policy Committee that they should seek to secure greater improvements for their members on or near basic rates and relatively little for members whose earnings are comparatively high, unions have, often after considerable efforts to establish a viable basis on which this can be done, either tacitly decided that it is not practicable—or have explicitly said that it would not be possible because of marked effect on differentials." This is partly because "unions and employers attach importance to adequate rewards for additional skill and responsibility".[2]

"The General Council considers that low-paid workers should continue to receive as much preferential treatment as practicable. This implies some narrowing of differentials. It would not, however, be realistic to expect those work people who are not in absolute terms low-paid to stand completely still. In some situations it may be necessary for special reasons to maintain or even, in exceptional circumstances, to widen existing differentials."[3]

Some unions have favoured solidarity as *between industries* in the form of tapering off increases for those industries in which earnings or productivity are above average, and granting relatively larger increases in less dynamic industries, for example, railways and the public services. This would compensate for higher drift in the former through higher rates in the latter. *But* implementation of such a policy presumes a degree of coordination within the TUC and within central employer organisations far beyond that which prevails today.

### "Solidarity" versus "Comparability"

The basic difficulty is that *the attempt to correct anomalies only perpetuates them.* A wage increase granted in the name of equity

---

[1] *Economic Review,* p. 72.
[2] *Ibid.,* pp. 69–70.
[3] *Ibid.,* p. 70.

stimulates a claim elsewhere on the grounds of "preserving existing differentials" or keeping rates "in line with each other". "Comparability" becomes leapfrogging and in the end the pattern of wage differentials is unchanged, but the level of money wages has increased.

The initial move may result from regrading, or merit rating, or additional incentives or a change in the system of PBR, or special bonuses. These promptly give rise to claims for increases elsewhere on grounds of equity, and the chain reaction is in process. Or the pressure may come from employers who are concerned not to let their effective wage rates fall out of line with those of their competitors in the same area for fear of losing their work force.

The concept of comparability has acquired a pervasive influence and an aura of tradition which are difficult to alter. It has come to be identified with the idea of "fairness", with the long established trade union principle of the "rate for the job". As such it is revered almost as a natural law. Workers tend to reject any effort to demote it as an attempt to force them personally to accept less pay than the next fellow—thus to bear the burden of wage restraint.

In the public sector the comparability principle has become official. It is considered to be necessary to enable the public services to attract and retain employees of high quality. And it has even been institutionalised in the form of a Civil Service Pay Research Unit with the purpose of making comparability studies. The investigations of this Unit into the wages paid for work in the private sector analogous to that done by civil servants form the basis for negotiations on pay in the public sector.

In the industrial civil service the pay structure is based upon "what is paid for a 40-hour week to time workers engaged in similar activities in outside employment". The Pilkington Commission and the Willinck Commission suggested methods of comparison for the medical and dental professions and for the police. For doctors and dentists and the higher civil service and the armed forces, independent review bodies have all worked on the basis of comparisons.

It was early in 1960 that the notion of "comparability" became enshrined as the "Guillebaud" principle. A three-man committee, with Mr. C. W. Guillebaud as chairman, was appointed by the

British Transport Commission and the three railway unions. Its task was to compare wage rates (not earnings) for jobs on the railways with similar jobs in other industries. The intention was that the findings were to be considered *along with other relevant considerations* as a basis for a mutually acceptable settlement. Events moved too swiftly, however, and an official strike precipitated a hasty completion and publication of the report. A settlement was reached on the basis of these findings alone without further discussion and negotiation.

From that time on the unions and the public have come to believe that the Guillebaud Report established a binding precedent entitling workers to pay increases automatically geared to upward movements in other industries. It is this concept which has largely accounted for the leapfrogging or ratchet pattern of wage bargaining.

*For example:* an increase in 1965 in the "M" rate which governs the pay of a large number of government industrial workers was derived in part from a December 1964 increase in the basic rate of the railway conciliation grades. The increase in the "M" rate in turn was one of the comparisons on which the railway unions then based *their* 1965 claim.

Thus each claim becomes a stepping stone to another in an inflationary wage-spiral. This attempt by an organised group of workers to maintain or improve its rank in the hierarchy of wages is necessarily self-defeating. And in the process it pushes up the whole level of money wages but not real wages.

The irony of the situation is that Mr. Guillebaud himself, in a letter to *The Times*[1], has stated that the Guillebaud report was a "once and for all exercise" and should not carry the interpretation put upon it by the unions. "I did not consider that in signing the report I was laying down a principle that would be valid for all time, irrespective of other relevant considerations. As an economist, and as one who has had much to do with wage negotiations, I hold that the continued application of the automatic principle of com-

---

[1] 28 January 1966.

parability would have an inflationary effect on wages in existing economic conditions."

## Productivity Bargaining and the Rate for the Job

One difficulty with productivity bargaining is that *it is incompatible with the solidarity principle of the standard rate for the job*

The essence of productivity bargaining is to relate wage increases to increases in efficiency in the particular plant achieved through changes in work practices. Productivity bargaining stimulates employers throughout industry to compete against each other in the effort to induce greater output through higher wages and benefits. In short, they are encouraged to pay significantly different rates for the same type of work.

This is a difficulty that is not always squarely faced. Indeed, there are some who will flatly deny that productivity bargaining conflicts with solidarity. And as evidence they will cite the obvious concern of productivity agreements—and of the NBPI in its various comments on productivity bargaining—with elimination of anomalies and inequities, with preferential treatment for low-paid workers, and with compensation for indirect workers who cannot directly participate in productivity agreements.

The point is that this genuine concern is in fact generated by the basic incompatibility of productivity bargaining with the rate for the job. This is not necessarily an indictment of productivity bargaining, since it has developed in response to quite a different problem. The purpose of productivity bargaining is to increase output and efficiency. It was not designed to tackle the problem of inequality in distribution of income from employment.

However, in the course of examining ways and means of increasing productivity in the work shop it was discovered that anomalies in wage structure have been an important cause of industrial unrest, restrictive work practices and inefficiency in production. Hence the catalogue of changes designed to improve manpower utilisation has attached high priority to overhauling of the wage structure *within* the plant.

These measures, which were described in Chapter IV, are of the utmost importance to efforts to achieve greater equity in income distribution. But this does not obviate the fact that it is inherent in the nature of productivity bargaining as it is presently conceived that it tends to distort the wage structure. This distortion is of two types: anomalies internal to plant or enterprise involved, and external anomalies which affect the wage structure of the industry. Both kinds of anomaly accentuate the "comparability" reflex.

*Productivity Bargaining and Internal Anomalies*

Productivity bargaining gives rise to pressures *within the plant or company concerned* for comparable wage increases to those workers who are not in a position to achieve any measurable increases in productivity. These may be "indirect" workers—mainly unskilled labourers—in ancillary services who feed the "direct" workers on production but are not immediately involved in the planned changes in work practices. Or they may be white-collar workers in clerical or administrative jobs, or supervisors whose pay may even be overtaken by raises to workers under them.

This engenders a sense of injustice, a resentment that rewards go to the less skilled or to those lucky enough to be in a position where it is possible to demonstrate increased productivity. If these internal "disturbances" are not taken into account, productivity bargaining will not be acceptable to work groups and to trade unions, and the increased efficiency will not be forthcoming. But how are internal disturbances to be taken into account?

The most forthright approach is to try to enforce the philosophy of solidarity underlying the Government's incomes policy. But this means that those in a position to make greater contributions to productivity must share part of their increase with those who are not in such a position.

This kind of "disturbance" arose in the case of the electrical supply industry which was reported on by the NBPI.[1] Manual workers and engineers were granted large pay increases in compensation for agreement to major changes in working practices. These included reduction in overtime payments, introduction of more flexible patterns of work and of hours, and the surrender of restric-

---

[1] NBPI Report No. 5.

tive practices. But in the case of administrative and clerical staff there were no major changes in working practices which would contribute substantially to greater output.

Nevertheless, the Board decided to recommend increases above the norm for the latter group in order to eliminate a "sense of disturbance which the efficient working of the industry requires should be reduced . . . we recognise that where greater changes in practice are required from some categories of workers in an enterprise than from others, with considerable accompanying changes in earnings, there can be left a sense of disturbance which must be reduced if the harmony of an enterprise is to be restored". This looks like an official plea for solidarity in the interest of efficiency!

This same principle of minimising disturbances was mentioned by the NBPI in its report on railworkers. For the lowest paid (clerical) grade of workers the Board recommended a 5 per cent increase. It went on to state that "account will have to be taken (by the proposed Pay and Productivity Councils) of those railway workers who, through no fault of their own, are unable to make a direct contribution to increased productivity by a change of working practice. . . ." Here a new kind of formula is hinted at in the suggestion that for such workers "pay should move in line with the average annual rate of increase in the national output per head".[1]

Another dimension of the problem is the Government's insistence that some part of the increased output should also be devoted to reductions in prices.

> The spread of productivity agreements is bound to be uneven. Ultimately most workers might hope to participate directly in them, but many will have to wait for years, and consumers who are not wage and salary earners, including pensioners, can only benefit through the effect on prices. Insistence through the policy that the gains shall be reflected in some degree to the consumer is the only way of ensuring that the gains are made available to everyone.[2]

But how are workers to be induced to accept far-reaching changes in the organisation of work and job content if at the same time they are asked to "give away" some of the reward to others who have not participated, including the consumer?

---

[1] *Loc. cit.*

[2] NBPI Report No. 36, p. 40.

The NBPI has clearly not found the solution to this dilemma in respect of productivity bargaining as it is now constituted. It points out that the basic difficulty lies in the disorderliness of the wage structure in the technological world of today.

> So long as the individual worker or group was relatively isolated in a simple system of production and the setting in which the work was done allowed incentives to work directly and without complication, the choice of a PBR system could be made with little regard for factors beyond those present in the immediate work situation. In the modern enterprise, however, with its complex pattern of grades, skills and wage rates, it is not possible to isolate the effect of payment systems in this way. Where no systematically agreed relationship between the wages of different grades is established and maintained, 'leapfrogging' pay claims are likely to result, and the entire establishment may be dragged into a condition of constant bargaining."[1]

The Board's approach to the dilemma is to conclude that *all* workers involved in the industry or enterprise must be compensated in order to avoid too great a disturbance of relativities. Indeed, most observers have stressed that productivity agreements must offer some benefit to everyone. The package must be made attractive enough to overcome all objections.

This conclusion is obviously endorsed by the trade unions. It is also the position of the Confederation of British Industry:

> . . . it is suggested that . . . where increases elsewhere in the plant are contemplated as a consequence of an agreement covering part of a plant, the cost of such increases should be borne by the savings resulting from the agreement in question. . . . Where . . . productivity agreements of wider scope are concerned, it is thought that it would be unfair for the probably substantial benefits to be enjoyed solely by employees who happen fortuitously to be in jobs which are directly affected by the changes taking place, and that where possible all employees should enjoy some share in the benefits of a productivity agreement.[2]

But the trouble is that this approach pushes up costs. This has been acknowledged by the NBPI in the sixth of its guidelines for productivity agreements which reads: "An agreement covering part of an undertaking should bear the cost of consequential increases elsewhere in the same industry if any have to be granted."

---

[1] NBPI Report No. 65, p. 31.

[2] Confederation of British Industry, *loc. cit.*, p. 9.

This is another way of saying that the "price" offered in return for changes in working practices must be high enough not only to induce the cooperation of workers directly involved, but also to compensate those *not* directly involved.

The productivity exception to the wage ceiling requires that productivity agreements must result, at least eventually, in lower unit costs. If this requirement is strictly administered, this higher "price" as a result of compensating indirect workers may act as a brake on the development of productivity agreements. And if the government is not this strict, higher costs of productivity agreements will put an additional inflationary strain on the incomes policy.

*Productivity Bargaining and External Anomalies*

There has been much discussion as to whether wage increases resulting from productivity agreements because they distort differentials in pay *as between firms in an industry,* are contagious and therefore inflationary. In the absence of proof positive on either side of the argument, about all that can be done is to list the arguments pro and con, and leave it to the reader to strike a balance.

Government spokesmen for the prices and incomes policies, and particularly the NBPI, not surprisingly take the position that productivity bargaining is not inflationary. This view is based largely on the argument that productivity agreements are designed to reduce unit costs, or at any rate to keep them from rising; and that wage increases that are offset by greater output need not increase prices.

Also it is pointed out that wage increases under a productivity agreement are expressly limited to workers covered by that agreement, and that demands for similar increases elsewhere in the industry will be granted only where they, too, are justified by the results of a productivity agreement or in terms of other criteria of the incomes policy.

Another argument is that individual employers will not be inclined to pass on, in the form of higher prices, wage increases resulting from a productivity agreement, since they cannot rely on competitors doing the same as they could in the case of nationally negotiated industry-wide increases.

Certainly the work of the NBPI so far corroborates its claim that an effort is being made to play down the role of comparisons in wage negotiations. It is true that comparability was given official acknowledgement as one of the criteria for wage increases under the incomes policy. But this was largely because it was not possible to ignore a criterion so deeply woven into the fabric of collective bargaining.

The criterion as laid down by the incomes policy provides for wage increases "where there is widespread recognition that the pay of a certain group of workers has fallen seriously out of line with the level of remuneration for similar work, and needs in the national interest to be improved".

The Board has clearly interpreted this as a demotion of the comparability principle insofar as it relates to detailed comparisons of basic rates (rather than earnings) in other industries. It emphasises that although the general principle of comparability will continue to apply, it will be given much less weight than hitherto.

Also a strict interpretation will be given to those words in the criterion which are in italics below: "where there is *widespread* recognition that the pay of a certain group of workers has fallen *seriously* out of line with the level of remuneration for *similar* work, and needs in the *national interest* to be improved."

Of particular importance is the stress on *similar work.* Prior to the advent of productivity bargaining no attempts had been made to evaluate the fairness of the wage rates which were being compared. And comparisons were often drawn between wage rates and earnings, for example, or between different degrees of skill, or between irrelevant or non-comparable time periods. On the general principle that statistics can prove anything, negotiations tended to be confrontations between two different sets of comparisons each more favourable to the side by which it was put forward. Much more attention will now be given to the validity of the comparisons drawn and to the necessity of comparing like with like.

Moreover, in the April 1968 White Paper on incomes policy, *Productivity, Prices and Incomes in 1968 and 1969,* it was emphasised that "The criterion justifying increases on grounds of comparability needs to be applied selectively, and must not be used to spread pay increases into areas of employment where the original justification does not apply."[1]

In its report on Productivity Bargaining, the Board stated that it has found no evidence to support the inflationary thesis. On the contrary, it claimed that the effect of major productivity schemes has been rather to stimulate other firms to negotiate their own agreements and thereby increase productivity. It adds: "Where a straight pay claim is put forward only on the ground that workers elsewhere have benefitted from productivity agreements, the company has good precedent for resisting it."[2]

Finally, it can be argued that productivity bargaining helps contain earnings drift and inflationary pressure by eliminating looseness in incentive payments and achieving more orderly wage structures.

This is an impressive defence of productivity bargaining with respect to the inflationary charge. There are many, however, who doubt that the force of comparability can be thus easily exorcised. And the doubters include both employers and trade unionists.

In its latest (May 1968) outline of its position on productivity bargaining the Confederation of British Industry states unequivocally: "However genuine plant productivity bargains may be, they will still tend to provoke unjustified claims elsewhere in the same industry or area and the higher pay agreed in a productivity bargain at plant level may quickly spread to other plants without being accompanied by the features of the bargain which relate to improvements in productivity."[3]

Therefore it insists that "while some increased payments must clearly accrue to workers directly affected by a productivity bargain, their resultant earnings should still be compatible with the general level of wages paid in a particular company for compar-

---

[1] *Loc. cit.*, para. 38.
[2] Report No. 36, p. 24.
[3] Confederation of British Industry, *loc. cit.*, p 11.

able jobs, since any great disparity would result in a series of leap-frogging claims".

A similar position is taken by the TUC. It has affirmed that it is "anxious to encourage genuine productivity and efficiency bargaining wherever possible".[1] But at the same time it cautions that "incomes policy will . . . remain vulnerable to the extent to which local bargaining itself provides a way of avoiding overall restraint. Even though only a minority of workpeople are in a position to enhance earnings in this way, and even though some of the increased earnings result from higher productivity or increased effort, *nevertheless this can and does stimulate claims from other groups based broadly on comparability arguments*." (Italics added.)[2]

Entrenched habits are notoriously difficult to change, and it is not realistic to expect trade unions to have much success in persuading their members to accept the disturbances to differentials caused by productivity bargaining without any attempt to "restore relativities". But one man's "anomaly" is another's "relativity", and the outcome is a chain reaction.

Indeed, the NBPI itself has argued in a number of places that undue fragmentation in bargaining results in anomalies which give rise to a sense of inequity and a consequent and never-ending struggle for adjustment which leads to inflation.

The fact that the comparability criterion for wage increases still stands on the books, no matter how cautiously phrased, makes it difficult to stem the tide of claims based upon it. This is particularly so in that it has been accepted that it is impracticable when negotiating a productivity agreement to postpone wage increases under it until the hoped-for productivity increases have materialised.

The effort required effectively to screen these claims and to uncover phoney bargains is probably beyond the resources of the government. And, indeed, since the success of the incomes policy

---

[1] TUC, *Economic Review*, 1968, p. 73.
[2] *Ibid.*, p. 27.

rests upon its voluntary character, there is no possibility of checking the comparability impulse without the full cooperation of both employers and trade unions.

Finally, with reference to the argument that productivity bargaining promotes greater orderliness in wage structure and thereby limits earnings drift, it is important to note that so far this has been true only *within* the plants or enterprises concerned. But the very process of rationalising the wage structure within a plant through a productivity agreement tends to pull it out of line with other plants in the same locality or the same industry. In short, plant productivity bargaining distorts the overall wage structure, thereby giving rise to secondary drift.

This has been recognised by the NBPI. In its report on the Engineering Industry it points out that a series of uncoordinated claims, negotiated without regard to the effect on other grades, leads to a pay structure for the industry which is always unsatisfactory, and thus to a constant attempt to push up the pay of those who seem to have fallen further behind.

Accordingly the Board appears to be moving in the direction of proposing that the role of national bargaining should be restricted to working out criteria for wage structure across industry, that is, to laying down criteria for relating the pay of one grade to that of another. Meanwhile the negotiation of wage increases should be left to local bargaining at plant level.

This is a complicated and controversial suggestion to which we shall return in the next chapter. But meanwhile it sheds interesting light on the inflationary dangers inherent in productivity bargaining at the plant level.

## Productivity Bargaining and Income Distribution

It bears repeating that the purpose of productivity bargaining is to improve manpower utilisation, increase productive efficiency and reduce unit costs of production. Therefore a book about productivity bargaining does not justify a full treatise on income distribution.

Still it is interesting how frequently the subject of "equity" crops up in the growing volume of literature on productivity bargaining. Whether the discussion is about restrictive work practices, comparability, drift, wage structure or obtaining worker assent to change, sooner or later it seems to revolve around concepts of "fair shares". This, then, is the excuse for a few passing observations on productivity bargaining and income distribution.

The first point relates to the difficulty of defining "equity". Most everyone is ready to declare himself in favour of *more* equitable distribution. Few, however, would subscribe to *absolute* equality. In between is the undefined, perhaps undefinable, no-man's land in which actual policy must operate. It may be possible to find a common denominator by stressing the need to link differentials with productivity; or to work towards similar pay for similar work; or to aim at solidarity by removing the more extreme differentials at the top and the bottom of the income scale; or even to attempt all three at once even though they are mutually incompatible.

But it is futile to search for any clearcut, unique, objective standard of equity to serve as a guideline. The most that can be hoped for is to move steadily *in the direction* of greater egalitarianism. There is no agreement as to how far one should ultimately move in that direction. But it *is* clear to most observers that the limit, however defined, is far removed. And it seems equally clear that the existing accidental, haphazard and disorderly income structure is so grossly unfair as to be unacceptable.

In any case it is academic to search for definitions. What matters is that those who participate in the working through of a productivity agreement, or of a prices and incomes policy, are fully conscious of the need for more equity. As George Brown put it in an exchange of correspondence with Maxwell Stamp:

"There is little hope of really getting folk to feel themselves involved in the business to such a degree that they accept in a personal way the obligations and responsibilities arising from it if at the same time they are vitally conscious of living in an unfair society where their just and in very many cases quite basic human requirements are inadequately provided for although others live very luxuriously indeed."

This concern over equity has a bearing on the attitude—sometimes subconscious—of many individual trade unionists to the concept of productivity bargaining. They are innately sceptical of proposals to *relate wage structure to productivity*. Partly this scepticism reflects their awareness of the inherent statistical difficulties in measuring productivity.

More fundamentally, however, it expresses their unwillingness to accept the existing pattern of income distribution. They don't like the assumption underlying productivity criteria for wage determination that the present wage structure is acceptable; that existing differentials accurately reflect what jobs are "worth" relative to each other; hence that starting from this base it is "fair" to reward increased effort or cooperativeness or efficiency with increased pay without otherwise altering wage structure.

This assumption is almost never made explicit. But workers sense what is happening. They sense it at the plant level where they are quick to object to increases granted—to the other fellow—under productivity agreements. And they sense it at the national level when it is proposed to hold overall wage increases within a norm determined by overall productivity. Here again they question the underlying assumption that the existing relation of employment income to income from profits and rents is the proper relationship which should be maintained *in perpetuum*. They point out that wages can increase, overall, faster than productivity and still not be inflationary—provided the net increase over and above productivity is "absorbed" by more progressive taxation, or higher savings or more competition and lower profit margins in industry.

More specifically this concern of some workers and business economists and government officials over income distribution thrusts itself into the arena of incomes policy and productivity bargaining in connection with *lower-paid workers*.

Most low-paid workers are women. The average earnings of men are just over £20 a week, but the average earnings of women are just under £10 a week. Also certain industries tend to be lower-paid than others. In agriculture, manual workers earn on average £13 12s. 6d. a week. In hats, caps and millinery, repair of boots and shoes, national government service and local government services the figure is between £15 and £16. And in clothing and parts of the textile industry it is about £17.

But low-paid workers can be found in every industry and in all parts of the country. Of 2,228 employees covered in the Ministry of Labour's family expenditure survey in September 1965 (up-date), 1.3 per cent were paid less than £12, 18 per cent less than £14, and nearly 33 per cent less than £16.

The concept of "minimum income" is becoming increasingly prominent in modern society. In the field of social insurance it operates through the programme for guaranteeing a minimum level of assistance to substandard income groups. In the field of earned incomes it is reflected in an effort to establish a minimum level for wages.

This same principle has been built into the prices and incomes policy. One of the four criteria for pay increases within the ceiling is "where there is general recognition that existing wage and salary levels are too low to maintain a reasonable standard of living".

The NBPI cannot itself guarantee an income floor for wage earners in line with reasonable standards of living. But if management and unions take the initiative in devising and negotiating agreed schemes for raising the incomes of lower-paid workers, and if these schemes are referred to the NBPI, the Board may then recommend that such exceptional increases are necessary to guarantee workers a reasonable standard of living.

There are various possibilities for applying such a policy of steady increases in minimum earned incomes. One such device is the "pro tanto" industry agreement designed to grant larger increases in lower wage brackets. In the three-year engineering agreement negotiated in 1964 it was provided that over the three years the level of minimum earnings would increase in six stages for those workers whose earnings for the normal week fell below the levels set out in the agreement. During the same period there would be only two general wage increases for all workers in engineering.

Thus a male labourer earning only the minimum rate would secure a 38-shilling advance over a three-year period, and labourers earning above the minimum level would only receive an additional 8 shillings a week. At the end of the period (1 January 1968) the minimum earnings guarantee level would become the minimum time rate.

In its report on the engineering workers published in December 1967,[1] the NBPI recommended a 15 per cent increase for some of the lower-paid employees comprising about one-seventh of the workers in the industry and no increase for the rest of the workers other than those granted in the context of productivity bargaining.

The TUC has proposed a minimum wage of £15 a week for a normal 40-hour week for all adult males. This would involve:

—the General Council seeking to secure from the CBI their broad agreement to the objective and their agreement to recommend it to employers' associations;

—negotiations at the level of particular industries between unions and employers, and possibly the establishment of joint teams to examine what improvements can be made in organisation, in the use of labour, and in wages structure with the specific aim of raising the production and earnings of lower-paid workers;

—and discussions with the government about the help that it can give in promoting this objective. One type of assistance might be government action on a selective basis to promote development in areas characterised by low earnings, and achievement of the objective might also involve enforcement action at a later stage at least in some industries.[2]

The CBI has explicitly rejected the suggestion of legislation on a national minimum wage.[3] And the two sides have agreed that they both need a great deal more information about the reasons for "low pay" where it exists in industry, and that they will wait for the findings of a government inquiry into the subject which is expected to be completed in 1969.[4]

Still another possibility for increasing minimum income levels for the lowest-paid workers would be a frontal attack on the problem of unequal pay for women. Such a proposal is currently

---

[1] NBPI Report No. 49, *loc. cit.*

[2] *Economic Review*, 1968, *loc. cit.*, p. 69.

[3] *Financial Times*, 2 April 1968.

[4] *Ibid.*

very much in the news. But again the TUC appears to shrink from direct action on the grounds that it would drastically alter differentials and increase total earnings and hence have a major inflationary effect.

This again reflects the ambivalent trade union attitude to the problems of differentials and solidarity which has been noted earlier. Mr. Woodcock, TUC General Secretary, is reported to have said that the incomes policies of the Government and the TUC could not go on indefinitely giving precedence to the pay claims of the "low paid". Higher-paid workers would eventually revolt against this scheme.[1]

It has been suggested by John Corina that

> A giant stride would be taken if the TUC committed itself to a policy of wage solidarity. The previous history of wage restraint shows that the success of any 'wage vetting' committee will depend on a clear principle involving self-restraint particularly on the part of the craft unions and the higher-paid. Unless this is forthcoming, it will be impossible to increase the rates and earnings of the low-paid without provoking demands by the higher-paid. . . . Unless the TUC itself lays down quantitative guidance . . . consultation with the unions will merely result in a competitive wage claim scramble to gain more than the norm.[2]

## Summary

In *theory,* trade unionists are committed to the principle of "solidarity", also known as "the rate for the job" or "equal pay for equal work". This implies a rational, orderly, consistent wage structure across industry, with differentials determined by the nature of the work rather than by commercial circumstances, profitability or the efficiency and negotiating strength of the individual worker or employer.

In *practice,* the actual wage structure is far from ideal in this sense, determined as it is by tradition, custom, the labour market, relative bargaining strength, incentive and bonus payments at the plant level, sectional rates of productivity growth, and the selective impact of technological change. It is characterised by inequities

---

[1] *Financial Times,* 2 April 1968.
[2] *The Development of Incomes Policy.*

and anomalies which generate inflationary wage drift through the process of comparability and leapfrogging.

Productivity bargaining can contribute to a more rational and equitable wage structure *within* a plant or enterprise. But it is essentially incompatible with the concept of solidarity or the standard rate for the job. Because it relates earnings to work practices in a particular plant, it results in differential rates for the same kind of work throughout an industry.

Productivity bargaining is designed as a way of increasing efficiency in utilisation of manpower, not of improving the distribution of income. Nevertheless, discussions on productivity bargaining inevitably entail consideration of "fair shares" because of the important bearing which workers' concern over equity has on their efficiency and their willingness to accept changes in working practices. Despite the difficulty of defining "equity", there is general agreement on the need for a more egalitarian wage structure. And there are many who are sceptical of the usefulness of productivity bargaining because of the difficulties of measuring productivity; and because it distorts pay differentials thereby exacerbating the problem of achieving a rational wage structure throughout the economy.

Chapter VII

# Productivity Bargaining and Collective Bargaining

## The Pattern of Collective Bargaining Machinery

The pattern of collective bargaining in the United Kingdom is a complex and overlapping network of plant, local, regional and national agreements. Formal negotiations between employers and unions are primarily national in scope, but actual earnings and conditions are increasingly determined more or less informally at the plant level.

The TUC, in its evidence to the Royal Commission on Trade Unions and Employers' Associations, divided industries into five classes according to the influence of industry-wide agreements on actual wages and salaries.[1] Some 30 per cent (seven million workers) are in industries where national industry-wide agreements are closely adhered to at company and local level. These include almost the whole of the public sector (national and local government, educational and health services and nationalised industries) as well as shipping, retail cooperatives and other services.

Another four million workers, or 17 per cent, are in Wages Council industries, including agriculture. Wages Councils fix minimum wage rates and conditions in industries where voluntary collective bargaining machinery is weak or non-existent. In most such cases wages are paid at or near the minimum.

Some six million workers, or 26 per cent, are in industries covered by industry-wide agreements but where company bargaining has an important influence on actual earnings. A little less than

---

[1] *Loc. cit.*, p. 10.

half of these six million are on PBR systems which are usually related to the national rate. Most of the rest are on time rates which are in some way related to earnings on PBR, e.g. through the "lieu" rates which are so common in engineering, shipbuilding, and iron and steel.

About one million workers, or 5 per cent, are covered by agreements implemented at company level, mainly by large non-federated employers. This category includes most productivity agreements.

Finally, there are some five million employees, or 22 per cent, who are not covered by any joint negotiating machinery. About half of the non-manual workers (for example, executives, supervisory staff, technicians, and clerical and administrative workers) as well as domestic servants, are in this group.

Thus according to these estimates some 14 million workers are covered by voluntary national negotiating machinery. About half of these are also covered by local or company bargaining and in most cases by national bargains as well.

The Royal Commission on Trade Unions and Employers' Associations has concluded, however, that the TUC groupings greatly underestimate the extent of influence exerted by local informal bargaining. This is because the earnings in many Wages Council industries and also in many public services tend to follow the pattern established by factory bargaining. In addition, even where rates fixed at industry level are fairly closely adhered to, more often than not they are supplemented by high levels of incentive earnings. "On any reasonable estimate the effective regulation of pay levels by industry-wide agreement is now very much the exception rather than the rule in Britain and is largely confined to the public sector."[1]

A recent Confederation of British Industry survey of its member employer organisations in most main industry groups indicated that in the majority of industries the weekly wage bill is determined by negotiations at both industry and plant level. But in more than two-thirds of the industries covered, industry level negotiations account for over 70 per cent of the weekly wage bill. In engineer-

---

[1] *Donovan Report*, p. 339.

ing, however, the contribution of plant level bargaining is "rather more than 30 per cent".[1]

The last Ministry of Labour survey of numbers of workers on PBR showed the following percentages in the main engineering sectors:

| | |
|---|---|
| Engineering and Electrical Goods | 47% |
| Marine Engineering | 63% |
| Vehicles | 52% |
| Metal Goods | 41% |

Usually bargaining to supplement industry-wide agreements takes place between managers and representatives of particular groups of workers. These representatives are ordinarily shop stewards; full-time union officers tend to be called in only in case of failure to agree. Workplace agreements are usually very informal. Many are not even written, and very few are collected together in a single coherent document.

## Bargaining at the National Level

A "national" agreement is an agreement between one or more employers' associations and one or usually more trade unions and it is intended to operate throughout an industry.

National agreements normally cover such issues as the length of the working week, the amount of paid holiday and regulations governing payment of extra allowances—for example, shift premia, overtime premia, payment for travelling time, etc. These are conditions which employers are anxious to have regulated nationally on a *standard* basis, not subject to improvement at the local level. They feel that since conditions of this kind raise production costs without being matched by increases in production, it is important that they should be standardised. Otherwise they might be used as competitive devices which could prove costly.

National industry-wide agreements also regulate pay. In this respect, however, they are much less standardised and less strictly adhered to at the local level.

[1] *Loc. cit.*, p. 3.

> Some fix only two time rates, one for skilled workers and another for unskilled, leaving individual firms to deal with intermediate and other grades. Others prescribe a list of different rates for a catalogue of different grades, with in addition a series of special additional payments for special duties or conditions of work. In industries in which a substantial number of women are employed, women are usually treated as forming a separate grade with rates of pay lower than those for unskilled men. Some agreements make no provision for payment by results; others do so, but in different degrees of detail. Some describe their rates as minimum rates, others as standard rates.[1]

The pattern of national collective bargaining represents an annual "wage-round" of a sort. Negotiations are bunched within relatively short periods at fairly regular intervals. There is a fair degree of uniformity as to size of increases within each round, but no precise timing as to the beginning and end. Most important agreements are concluded in the winter or early spring, with a few in the smaller industries dragging on until the summer, or even autumn. The majority of collective agreements are "open-ended", that is, of no specified duration so that their reopening is a matter of strategy and tactics.

The wage-round pattern, such as it is, is also influenced by certain key industries or pace-setters. These bear a definite relation to size of payroll. For instance, the most important pace-setter, the engineering industry, employs directly some two and a half million workers, and indirectly affects the wage levels of another one and a half million. The railways, which employ about 600,000 also have had an important influence.

On the other hand, negotiations in the construction industry, which employs one million directly and indirectly, usually occur in February, and hence they tend to follow rather than set the pace. Coal mining, although it engages nearly 400,000 workers, has tended to be regarded as a special case which does not necessarily provide a precedent for other industries. Similarly, although the printing industry is one of the most powerful bargainers because of its "control of the job" based on special skills, its structure is too different from that of other industries to serve as a pattern.

---

[1] *Donovan Report*, p. 13.

The annual wage-round pattern is being altered by a recent trend towards longer-range, fixed-term agreements covering two-and-a-half to four years. Such agreements have been concluded for printing, heating and ventilating, boots and shoes, matches, tobacco, gas, electrical contracting and electrical supply, building, some sectors of engineering and others. Most of them provide for "annual improvement factors" resulting in periodic rate increases related to projected growth in productivity.

National bargaining has been woven—probably inextricably—into the fabric of British industrial relations. There were substantial reasons why the pattern of bargaining developed as it did. And these reasons are just as forceful today as they ever were. Hence it is fallacious blithely to assume—as do many observers of the current scene—that national bargaining is obsolete and in the process of disappearing.

*What do employers, and particularly employers' federations, like about national bargaining?*

In the inter-war years of depression and unemployment a major motive for the development of national bargaining was the concern of employers to prevent wage cutting by their competitors. Subsequently, and still today, they have been anxious to standardise wage levels in order to prevent "whipsawing". This is the process by which trade union bargaining pressure is applied at the local level to particularly vulnerable employers. The objective is to force wage concessions that other employers in the area and the industry will eventually have to meet in order to retain their workers. In essence this is the well-known tactic of "divide and conquer".

"Whipsawing" is more than a transitional phenomenon. In the United States where collective bargaining is almost altogether conducted on the plant level, it is very common. And even in Britain it continues to be a serious threat on the contemporary industrial scene. One of the most graphic descriptions of "whipsawing" appears in a NBPI report published at the end of 1967.

> . . . the staff unions (in engineering), in particular D.A.T.A. . . . have followed the policy of using the negotiating procedure to pursue at domestic and district level numerous claims of an identical kind which had from time to time been the subject of discussion at national level without agreement being reached. If these claims have not been met,

> official strike action has been approved in selected cases. Companies generally have been chosen for such action because of their commercial vulnerability at a point in time. Once a few firms have made the desired concessions other firms have been more easily convinced to do likewise under threat of similar treatment. The classic use of this strategy was by D.A.T.A. in pursuing its claim for increased annual holidays. It was the success of these tactics which prompted the (Engineering Employers') Federation to propose the charter which would have ruled out domestic bargaining on conditions. The union's tactics can be fairly said to have been a response to the Federation's tactics, which were designed to limit the scope and importance of national bargaining and thereby contain union demands and restrict their influence.[1]

A closely related reason for preferring national to local bargaining is the fact that employers can multiply their negotiating strength by pooling their separate efforts. By centralising negotiations at the national or district level, they avoid the weakness and diffusion that result from fragmented bargaining. They also compound their effectiveness *vis-à-vis* national union. This enables them to keep wages lower than they otherwise might be.

Employers themselves tend to phrase these advantages of national bargaining in terms more judicious than "bargaining power" or avoiding "whipsawing". As the CBI puts it:[2]

> Collective bargaining at national level has made, over the years, an important contribution to the maintenance of stability in the wages system. . . . It has been able to provide some check on excessive wage settlements at local level and it may be said that without national collective bargaining the rate of inflation in the economy would have been greater. It has prevented . . . the indiscriminate forcing up of the price of labour with its damaging long-term effects on the general economy of the country. . . . (it) provides a useful means whereby a measure of control can be exercised by the trade unions over their local officials and whereby individual employers can be deterred from making local concessions which are likely to prejudice the position of employers generally in the same industry.

In addition, employers feel that national bargaining provides effective dispute machinery and tends to reduce strikes. They also appreciate the economy of time and effort involved in substituting one negotiation at national level for hundreds of local agreements. And they value the setting up at national level of a framework for

---

[1] Report No. 49, p. 7.

[2] *Loc. cit.*, pp. 4–5.

regulating wage structure. Although employers favour wage differentials which accurately reflect variations in skill, effort and qualifications, they too, like trade unions, see the necessity of exercising some control over the range of differentials in the interest of an orderly, consistent wage structure which can effectively respond to market forces.

These at least are the advantages which employers profess to see in centralised national bargaining. But at the same time it is quite clear that they like standardisation of wages and conditions only in relation to *formal* collective agreements with trade unions.

Individually, however, with reference to pay and conditions for his own workers, each employer is more likely to claim the right to deviate from the standard. Perhaps the feature about national bargaining that employers favour most is the *flexibility* which it gives them for unilateral and informal differentiation at the plant or enterprise level. Within the collective bargaining framework established through national negotiations they feel free to adjust and supplement national rates and conditions to meet their particular needs and according to their particular capacity to pay; and at their own discretion without the rigidity of contractual commitment or trade union interference. Also since the national agreement relates largely to minimum standards, this affords protection to the marginal employers who cannot afford to pay more than this minimum.

Certainly in recent years national agreements have been widely supplemented by local workshop agreements with shop stewards in response to particular pressures in the plant and in the area. These agreements are neither explicit nor formal. On the contrary, they are usually undocumented and are sufficiently loose and vague to give employers the flexibility they want for meeting competition for labour, satisfying local claims, setting up incentive schemes, and adjusting wages and working conditions to the special needs of the plant and the area.

Employers feel that such informal practices give them more discretion and constitute less of a restriction on their prerogatives. They do not establish precedent and are reversible with the turn of the business cycle. They are less likely to lead to strike action or whipsawing tactics. And they are less offensive to employers' associations whose protection they value and whose officials are likely to frown on individual bargaining.

*Trade unions, too, attach great importance to national bargaining.* In part this is for reasons similar to those which motivate employers. In years of economic depression they, too, want protection against competitive wage cutting. They value the kind of orderliness and rationality in the wage structure that can only be achieved and regulated at the national level across firms, industries and geographical areas. They find that centralised national bargaining is less of a strain on their slender resources of skilled negotiators than fragmented bargaining at plant or company level. They rely on the bargaining strength which stems from pooling their negotiating efforts and presenting a common front backed by the threat of strike action over a broad sector of industrial activity. And they appreciate the freedom which is left them by national bargaining to exploit to the full local labour shortages which enable them to raise actual earnings above the national minima.

But the major reason for trade union attachment to national bargaining is their basic tenet of *solidarity.* This is an objective that can only be pursued on an industry-wide basis. It is only through the pressure of external bargaining on a national scale that there is any hope of narrowing differentials, of making them more rational, of ensuring the "rate for the job", or improving wages for lower-paid workers, and of protecting workers in small plants from unfavourable settlements.

And yet, despite this attachment of employers and of trade unionists to the principle of national bargaining, it is now freely admitted on both sides that national bargaining has failed to achieve what was expected of it. It has not effectively determined either the level or the structure of wages or fringe benefits. It has not brought order or rationality or equity into the wage structure and has certainly not established "the rate for the job". It has failed to stabilise industrial relations and to prevent strikes. It does not provide a framework in which wages can be related to productivity in any meaningful or quantifiable way. By permitting work groups to exercise through workshop sanctions what amounts almost to "illicit" control over earnings, it has eroded both managerial prerogatives and the influence of trade unions over their members. It has failed to elicit worker cooperation in technical change, removal of restrictive practices and redeployment of labour. And it has not prevented—on the contrary, it has contributed to—wage drift, inflation and consequent checking of economic growth.

### Bargaining at the Local Level

The most striking feature of collective bargaining in the post-war period has been the shift in the centre of gravity from national negotiations to the workshops. Much of the size and shape of the pay packet is now settled at the plant level. This happens partly within the framework of nationally negotiated agreements, but largely independently of them.

The effect has been to increase considerably actual earnings above the level of basic wages specified in national agreements. For example:

—in shipbuilding, only about 5 per cent of the craftsmen receive the basic rate only;

—in engineering, only about 2 per cent of skilled workers receive only the minimum rate;

—in printing, nearly all workers get something on top of the basic rate; and

—in multiple retailing, it is estimated that about half the workers get more than the national minimum.

This change in the level set by national bargaining is usually accomplished indirectly. It may be achieved by revising piecework rates; or by altering the wage structure; or by increasing overtime; or by upgrading and promotion; or by special payments in the form of incentive bonuses like merit rates and compensation for dirty work or exposure to rough conditions. Sometimes it is done more directly by "filling in the details" of broad national agreements. Or firms may openly grant wages above the nationally agreed level for the industry—most often on the grounds of "comparable" wages paid elsewhere.

Many factors have contributed to this extension of the bargaining process to the workshop floor. They include the growing influence of shop stewards, the involvement of works management in grievance procedures, the growth of personnel management, and the greater awareness and sophistication of both supervisors and trade union officials in the field of industrial relations techniques.

But the basic reason lies in the fact that any given industry—and particularly the engineering industry which accounts for well over 10 per cent of the total work force—is too diverse within itself to allow of industry-wide standardisation. An industry comprises a large number of firms of different sizes, dealing with a variety of products, utilising many different kinds of technology and equipment and productive methods, and operating in different geographical regions subject to local variations in supply and demand for labour and raw materials. Hence it is not possible at national level to negotiate much more than key minimum rates and general guidelines for differentials, working hours, fringe benefits and shift premia. A great deal has to be left to company and plant bargaining.

It is at the plant level that the effects of changing technology make themselves felt. Technical change can be planned outside the workplace, but it can only be executed *within* it. The most common unit for change is not the industry, or even the company, but most often the group of workers in the factory or office or department. At this level the initiative, the decision as to whether change takes place or not, rests almost entirely with management.

Hence it is at the plant level that the most vital decisions affecting workers are taken. These include lieu rates, application of job evaluation and of incentive payment schemes, the granting of special payments and bonuses, distribution of work loads, allocation of overtime, promotion, staffing, transfer, discipline, sick benefits, facilities for shop stewards, redundancy, etc. Even more significant, many of the obstacles to efficient use of labour can only be removed by action close to the shop floor; for example, the level of overtime differs greatly between firms and would be expensive to "buy off" right through the industry. Similarly, demarcation rules are often the product of local circumstances or local history, and are not embodied in union rules. There are other issues which are regulated nationally only in terms of minimum conditions or standards, but are actually determined locally; for example, piece-work prices or terms, other bonus payments, and overtime payments. And it is only at plant level that changes in pay can be related to changes in work performance.

Thus most of the benefits obtained by workshop negotiations are not in contravention to national agreements but are supplementary to them. Moreover, it would be difficult to cover them at the national level. In general plant bargains do not conflict with national agreements. Rather they deal with issues that are not covered in national agreements.

We have already noted the preference of employers for this kind of informal workshop bargaining supplementary to national agreements. They like it because it is largely undocumented, because negotiations are with shop stewards and/or work groups rather than directly with external trade union officials, and because it rests primarily on custom and practice. Thus it keeps disputes within the firm, avoids contractual commitments, provides maximum flexibility and detracts little from "managerial prerogative".

The preference of employers for informal and unwritten arrangements was investigated in some detail by the research director of the Royal Commission on Trade Unions and Employer Associations. His findings have been summarised as follows: [1]

> If agreements were formalised they would become established *de jure* rights which could not be withdrawn; even if existing stewards would not abuse formal confirmation the next generation might, and managers like to believe that they can vary privileges according to the response they get; once the process of formalising began it would extend indefinitely; and, finally, 'some *de facto* concessions could not be written down because management, particularly at board level, would not be prepared to admit publicly that they had been forced to accept such modifications in their managerial prerogatives and formal chains of command'. The more concessions are made the stronger become all these reasons for preferring informality.

---

[1] *Donovan Report, loc. cit.*, p. 28.

On the whole, employer associations have acquiesced—however reluctantly—in this shift of real power from the industry to the plant level.

Partly this has been because of their impotence to do otherwise.

> In most industries industry-wide agreements cannot deal effectively with these issues because individual companies have not delegated authority to settle them to their associates, and they have no intention of doing so now. Even if they were willing it would make no difference, for variations between firms in size, management structure, management policies, technology and market situations would defeat any attempt to exercise detailed control over most of these issues from outside the firm.[1]

In some cases, however, employers' associations have not been interested in controlling the actual level of remuneration. They feel that the individual employer is a better judge of his particular labour market and manpower needs. Hence they find it more comfortable not "to take on the thankless task of trying to enforce decisions over their members who are also their masters. They can devote their time to more manageable tasks."[2]

These more manageable tasks include using their influence—through exhortation, advice, information, assistance and propaganda—to try to persuade their members not to arrive at settlements likely to "embarrass" each other.

At the same time, however, employers' associations appear to be uneasy about the shift to plant bargaining and its eroding effect on their own influence and authority. And they are currently in search of ways of reasserting that authority and strengthening their grip on collective bargaining.

Trade unions, too, are uneasy about the shift of bargaining power to the shop floor.

They clearly recognise the various reasons why decisions need to be taken at plant level. As the TUC puts it:[3]

> In most cases productivity bargaining has to be done at company or plant level if the action to be taken to improve efficiency is to be adequately defined, and if the benefits to the work people are to be

---

[1] *Donovan Report, loc. cit.*, p. 40.
[2] *Ibid.*, p. 33.
[3] *Economic Review, loc. cit.*, 1968, pp. 26, 28.

related closely enough to the actual effects of changes on the job. . . . Economic progress will not be secured by general policies. . . . Must translate the nation's interest into action at the level of the particularly individual and the individual firm.

But they are not blind to the fact that plant bargaining has weakened their influence over their members. As a result of wage drift and the proliferation of piecework, bonuses, premia and fringe benefits, actual earnings are increasingly determined at the plant level—and more often than not unilaterally by management. Workers are well aware of this trend; hence they tend to lose interest in trade unions as the channel for obtaining higher incomes and living standards. Over the past decade trade union membership has actually declined relative to labour force.

Insofar as managements do bargain at the plant level on organisation and remuneration of work, they tend to negotiate with shop stewards or direct representatives of work groups rather than with outside trade union officers. Where agreements are reached at shop steward level without difficulty, district officers as well as officials of employer federations, do not interfere.

The Donovan Report points out[1] that "since there are probably about 175,000 stewards in this country, compared with perhaps 3,000 full-time trade union officers, this suggests that shop stewards must be handling many times the volume of business conducted by their full-time officers". This "business" may include various aspects of pay, level and distribution of overtime, shift working, disciplinary issues, distribution of work, pace of work, manning of machines, job transfers, grievances, introduction of new machinery and new jobs, taking on of new labour and redundancy.

The decline in trade union membership as a share of the labour force has been partly due to structural shifts and the relative increase in numbers of white-collar workers, who are less interested in joining unions. Partly also it is a consequence of full employment which enhances the workers' sense of security and reduces their feeling of dependence on the unions. But even more it is the result of the earnings drift and ineffective trade union organisation at plant level. Workers attribute improvements in earnings and in

---

[1] *Donovan Report, loc. cit.*, p. 26.

working conditions either to unilateral concessions by employers or to efforts of shop stewards who have only very loose ties to trade unions, rather than to trade union officials.

In theory the average union member has two points of contact with his union, one in the shop with his shop steward or with the local branch official on his visits to the shop; the other at meetings of his branch union. In practice, however, both kinds of contact have proved ineffective for making the worker union-conscious.

The worker tends to identify the union with the person of his shop steward who collects union dues, disseminates information on union activities, and deals directly with the employer on grievances, wage rates and working conditions. But the shop steward may have only a loose relation with the trade union. Membership in trade union branches is based on residence rather than place of work. The average branch union official has many firms in his area. He has innumerable responsibilities and little staff and equipment for meeting them. This means that he can visit particular firms only very infrequently. He most certainly cannot familiarise himself with the special situation in that plant or with the individual workers.

Local branch meetings do little to fill this gap. This is primarily because workers know that branch officials have so little impact on actual wages and working conditions. It is also a result of the normal apathy apparent in most organisations in the modern world with its many distractions, including particularly TV and motor cars.

The General Secretary of the TUC, George Woodcock, is fully aware of this creeping malaise in trade unionism. At the 1965 TUC Congress he said from the platform:

> I will tell you flatly to your faces, you will go through the motions as unions and you will boast yourselves as unions, and already many of your members are getting three times as much as you have negotiated for them. . . . The trade union movement is being transformed, if not eroded, because of your lack of control already.

## Productivity Agreements and Two-tier Bargaining

The rapid development of productivity agreements has intensified and focussed the debate over national versus plant bargaining. In particular it has underlined that *bargaining should take place at the level where key decisions are made.*

The outcome has been a much clearer understanding of the need for plant bargaining. It is only at the plant level that certain vital issues can be tackled. Only at this level is it feasible for the work system to be precisely analysed. It is only at this level that there is real scope for the meaningful and protracted consultation which is essential to effective productivity bargaining. It is here that unified management is available and capable of participating in consultations and taking the required decisions. It is at the local level that management can commit itself to specific changes which take account of the distinctive features of the workplace. And it is only at this level that concessions to workers can be linked with productivity and labour utilisation.

This is the situation in most of private industry. But still there is some room for industry and company productivity agreements, and a fair number of them have been concluded. The more centralised an industry, the less scope there is for shop floor bargaining. For example, in the Post Office and on the railways really important collective agreements are signed at the national level. But in engineering and printing where local circumstances vary considerably, national agreements fix only minimum rates and conditions over a fairly narrow range of subjects. The degree of centralisation differs greatly as between industries, depending on traditional relations between individual plants and the central body.

It has, however, become abundantly clear that productivity bargaining is a more complicated exercise on an industry-wide basis. Consultation and communication are more difficult over such a large area. There are problems in identifying industry-wide obstacles to greater efficiency and even more in devising effective means of removing them. Enforcement problems are compounded and much greater demands are made on negotiating officials on both sides. Hence it is not surprising that many of the industry-wide productivity agreements—for example, electricity supply—have been of the "statement of intent" type and have been supplemented by detailed local agreements at plant level.

A problem arises in connection with productivity bargaining for plants in multi-plant and multi-industry firms. Although the individual plants may be working under quite different conditions and for different markets, there is centralisation at the firm level of decisions on investments, financing, pricing and cross subsidisation which have an important bearing on plant bargains. Hence effective productivity bargaining requires that approximations or notational estimates be worked out on a plant basis; many firms do this already. This is why some firms, for example British Oxygen, ICI and Esso Distribution, have engaged in a kind of two-tier bargaining, i.e., central bargaining at firm level on minimum terms and supplementary rates to be determined at plant level.

Thus many factors point in the direction of plant level bargaining. At the same time, however, it is significant that most of the vital issues arising at plant level *have implications for industrial relations that cut across various firms in an industry and various industries in the economy.* For both employers and trade unions it is important that the general principles relating to these issues should be incorporated into collective agreements at a level higher than the individual enterprise. This is essential in order to:

—safeguard the strength of trade unions and employer associations which flows from coordination and pooling of individual bargaining power;

—protect the concept of solidarity and standardisation of wage rates and working conditions; and

—alleviate managerial fears of whipsawing and pressure on marginal firms.

Clearly the attempt to take account of both of these factors—the need for bargaining at the local level and for coordination at a higher level—must involve some form of two-tier bargaining. This two-tier bargaining can be based on the principle that agreements reached in the workshop should be articulated with, and made part of, more comprehensive formal collective agreements at a higher level.

What are the possible mechanisms for achieving two-tier bargaining? A large number of proposals have been made in various places by various observers. For convenience they can be grouped under three headings:

A. Broader Scope for Collective Bargaining at the National Level
B. More Influence for National Organisations at Plant Level
C. National Bargaining for Minimum Standards; Plant Bargaining for Increases.

A. *Broader Scope for Collective Bargaining at the National Level*

There are a number of important issues which so far have barely been touched upon in national agreements which might well be brought more prominently into the collective bargaining framework at that level. For these issues the national agreements might well lay down *guidelines* and *minimum standards* for an industry or specified section thereof. This is feasible insofar as there are aspects which are common throughout the industry or sector irrespective of size of firm, stage of technology, geographic location, etc. The result would be a national framework within which details could be determined by supplementary negotiations at plant level.

Issues which might lend themselves to such "guideline" national negotiations include overall levels of overtime, shift work, principles of PBR systems, work study and measurement, job evaluation, intercraft flexibility, merging of white-and blue-collar status, setting of limits to differentials and protection of low-paid workers, training programmes and redundancy benefits and requirements.

On redundancy, as an illustration, it should be possible in a national agreement to standardise for an industrial sector formal notice periods, relocation allowances and wage maintenance payments in case of transfer, and levels of severance pay. Indeed, the agreement might go so far as to draw up a "model" redundancy agreement as a basis for schemes at the firm level. These might be subject either to collective bargaining procedure at that level or to unilateral adoption by the firm.

This kind of *statement of minimum requirements* should be possible for each of the issues listed above, and for many others. The result would be a greater degree of standardisation and coordination throughout the industry without sacrifice of the essential flexibility required at plant level.

A much more ambitious proposal is that the broad *guidelines for, and overall supervision of, productivity bargaining* in an industry should be determined by national agreement. Actual agreements would be hammered out at local level but *within* the guidelines laid down nationally.

This kind of integration of local and national machinery for productivity bargaining has been advocated by the CBI, by the TUC and by the National Board for Prices and Incomes. In the words of the latter:

> . . . the best course for an association to follow would in our view be to issue guidelines . . . modified to suit the industry's own circumstances. Members would be expected to observe these in any productivity agreements they might sign, and would otherwise observe the existing agreements. The association would follow negotiations closely, register the resulting agreements and circulate information to other members.[1]

Such an approach could prove relatively innocuous if guidelines were drawn in very general terms. On the other hand, the proposal carries within it a potential for developments of far-reaching significance. Very little detail has been forthcoming about the possibilities of using such national guidance for supervising and coordinating *the wage structure* of an industry. But suppose the industry negotiators were charged with:

—trying to eliminate wage anomalies as between firms in the industry;

—or compressing or limiting differentials within the industry;

—or altering the wage structure of the industry in favour of lower-paid workers, i.e. asking some firms to hold back on wage increases while others increased their wage levels.

This would mean that officials from organisations external to the firm—employers' associations and trade unions—would be entitled to restrict management's freedom in negotiating on domestic issues

[1] Report No. 36, *loc. cit.*, pp. 36–37.

which have long been considered to be subject to "managerial prerogative". And if the exercise were carried to its logical conclusion, the objective would become that of rationalising wage structure *throughout the economy*. This would involve eliminating anomalies as between industries, compressing wage differentials throughout industry, and asking some industries to exercise wage restraint for the sake of above-average increases in others. It may well be asked what body of officials would take decisions of such proportions, to say nothing of how they would be enforced.

B. *More Influence for National Organisations at Plant Level*

In any case, even if carried to this extreme, it is clear from much that has already been said that national negotiations can never completely usurp the field of collective bargaining. The current preoccupation of organisations on both the employer and the trade union side is to find ways of increasing their leverage at plant level.

Much of the importance of productivity bargaining lies in its usefulness for this purpose. Productivity bargaining procedure is quite distinct from conventional collective bargaining. Conventional bargaining is mostly on the national level between employer federations and national trade union officials; productivity bargaining requires consultation at plant level even when the final agreement is with a company or an entire industry.

Before the advent of productivity bargaining, negotiations at the plant level were informal, not embodied in contracts. They usually were nothing more than an "understanding" with shop stewards.

But productivity bargaining is changing the traditional concept of managerial prerogatives by recognising that change can be made acceptable only with the consent of employees. It cannot be imposed on them.

> Productivity agreements involve the acceptance by management of the principle that workers have rights of a certain value vested in a particular pattern of work and that these rights can with advantage be bought out at an economic price.[1]

---

[1] National Board for Prices and Incomes, Report No. 36, *loc. cit.*

This in turn makes industrial relations more formal and more specific at the plant level. Proposed changes in work practices are made explicit. They are precisely defined in a written agreement signed by national trade unions. And they are actively administered according to agreed procedures. Thus basic issues are removed from one-sided managerial discretion and brought into the formal framework of collective bargaining.

But if productivity bargaining is an *opportunity* for national organisations to enhance their influence at local level, it is also a *challenge*. Major structural changes are required in both employer associations and in trade unions if such intervention is to be effective.

1. *Trade Unions*

The diversity and untidiness of British trade union structure can probably not be matched elsewhere in the world. There are some 574 separate unions with a membership of 10,111,000. Unions vary in size from the the 24 members of the Jewish Bakers' Union to the 1,482,000 members of the Transport and General Workers' Union.

But the organisational structure is somewhat less disorderly than these figures might indicate. Of the total number of members, one-half are in the nine largest unions, and four-fifths are in the thirty-eight largest unions. Only 170 unions are affiliated to the TUC, but these include a total membership of nearly 9 million employees.

On the other hand it is virtually impossible to describe the movement in terms of neat categories or types of union. Many are "craft" unions and a few are "industrial", but the majority are "multi-craft" or "general" or "occupational". And even these definitions are difficult to describe in any consistent or concise way. In the words of the Donovan Report, the biggest of the unions "have achieved their position by linking together groups and sub-groups of workers from different industries and services in patterns of astounding complexity which can be given historical explanations, but yield to no logical interpretation".[1]

---

[1] *Loc. cit.*, p. 30.

Roughly the dividing lines are somewhat as follows. A "craft" union comprises workers possessing a certain skill or range of skills; for example, the United Pattern Workers Association. An "industrial" union comprises all workers in a given industry; for example, the National Union of Railwaymen or the National Union of Mineworkers. A "multi-craft" union includes only the skilled or semi-skilled workers in an industry and possibly also some crafts in other industries; for example, the Amalgamated Engineering Union. The two large "general" unions—the Transport and General Union and the National Union of General and Municipal Workers—include a mixed group of semi-skilled and unskilled workers cutting across industries. "Occupational" unions cover non-craft occupations—such as clerical workers—in a number of industries.

This diversity of union structure has created a problem of multi-unionism which enormously complicates plant level bargaining. Investigations have shown that "even if white-collar workers and their unions are left out of account, about four out of every five trade unionists in Britain work in a multi-union establishment, and perhaps one in six of them belongs to a grade of workers in which two or more unions are competing for members".[1]

This difficulty, in turn, is linked with what has come to be known as the "shop steward problem". In Britain, some 175,000 shop stewards, more or less, perform tasks that on the Continent are largely taken care of by works councils or committees, and in the United States by detailed plant agreements negotiated with trade union locals. The shop steward's function in relation to management is to speak on behalf of the members of his union who are employed in the shop. He provides a recognised point of contact between management and employees, particularly in negotiations affecting earnings and conditions of work. He may also assist in settling complaints and disputes between workers and management according to procedures agreed by the industry's joint negotiating body.

Shop stewards operate nominally as part of trade union structure, but their ties to the union have been steadily loosening. Trade union rules and procedures with respect to shop stewards were devised

---

[1] *Ibid.*, p. 29.

many decades ago, and are not adapted to modern industrial structure. They are too vague to give much actual guidance, and they are frequently honoured in the breach.

Another basic difficulty is that the local unit of the trade union is the branch based upon geographic location rather than on place of work. Branch trade union officials are too few, too poorly paid and equipped and too busy to visit particular plants more than infrequently. They seem never to be in the right spot at the right time. And few workers attend branch meetings.

More important, since there are usually several unions represented in a firm, any one union speaks for only a fraction of the workers. Each of the union groups within the plant will normally be represented by a shop steward. These in turn may form a committee and elect a shop convenor or chairman, and in some cases make contact with similar committees in other firms.

Workers in the shop regard the steward as their representative, rather than their union branch official, and they think of wage increases as stemming from his efforts. Actually, negotiated increases in the national rate do influence local rates by setting a minimum, and in many cases by being added to local rates when these are already above the minimum. But the average worker does not realise this. He never sees the national leaders who are negotiating what he considers to be minima that do not apply to him.

Thus there is a sharp break in internal trade union communications between officials and members. Executive authority flows down to the branch, but the flow of bargaining activities in the shop goes through the steward. And there is almost no connection between the two points. The shop convenor or joint committee of stewards may be loosely accredited to a federation of unions. Sometimes they even set up "combine committees" of leading stewards in each plant belonging to a multi-plant enterprise.

None of these efforts, however, succeeds in overcoming the basic problem that there is no *one* member organisation to which the shop steward reports and is responsible. As a result stewards are inclined to soft-pedal union loyalties in favour of shop loyalty. This is due partly to the nature of their task and the need to cooperate with other stewards on plant norms. Moreover, each steward is confronted by two sets of rules, those of his own union and the uniform set of rules or procedures for the shop agreed upon by the various unions with the employer. Thus he finds it difficult to obey all of the rules all of the time, or to wait for instructions from above in each of the many situations that arise daily.

These developments carry with them the danger of degeneration into "private" plant unionism which could deprive national unions of their grip over collective bargaining. Not surprisingly shop stewards sometimes take independent action which exceeds their jurisdiction as loosely defined by national agreements or outdated union rules. Nor is it surprising that multi-union work groups come to regard themselves as self-governing organisations or "private unions within a union".

This shop floor view of the workers' organisation in the plant as a self-governing association is in contrast to the formal rule book view under which the primary unit of union organisation at workshop level is regarded as but a minor and subordinate part of the trade union. Thus the influence of the trade unions over their members is considerably diluted at the plant level. This loosening of the union "grip" clearly makes it more difficult to negotiate acceptable productivity agreements or to carry out a rational prices and wages policy.

At the same time, however, the complexity, formality and explicit nature of productivity agreements have in many cases brought trade unions more prominently into negotiations and forced shop stewards to coordinate more closely with them. This is particularly the case where negotiations are conducted at company level. This development seems to have had some impact on the shop steward attitude of independence. In some instances shop stewards have disagreed with union officials during the negotiations, but generally they have had to give way.

The NBPI has concluded that productivity bargaining has helped to solve some of the problems of workshop negotiation stemming from trade union structure in that it has encouraged unified negotiations. Practically all productivity agreements have been concluded with more than one union. This eliminates a good deal of leapfrogging.

There have been a spate of proposals for integrating shop stewards more closely with trade unions. These have included:

—putting shop stewards on a paid basis with more time and more facilities for union duties and more adequate protection against being fired;

—more adequate supervision of shop stewards by trade union officials, which implies more and better paid officials; according to the Donovan Report "there are about 3,000 full-time trade union officials in Britain, which represents about one union official for every 3,800 trade union members. Equally reliable figures are not available for all other comparable countries, but the evidence suggests that in the United States the ratio of officers to members is of the order of 1 to 1,400 and in the Federal Republic of Germany as low as 1 to 800. Both Italy and France appear to have twice as many officers per member as we do".[1]

—more adequate training for shop stewards and for trade union officers. It is coming to be recognised that trade union expertise can have a major influence on managerial decisions. In Sweden and Germany trade union officials have had to specialise, and at the workshop level trade union representatives have become versed in production techniques, work study, factory safety measures, ergonomics, bio-technical studies, occupational studies, industrial hygiene, business economics, business administration and personnel management, and

—providing local trade union officials with better information and technical and professional facilities from national unions, including financial analysis, accounting, sociological and economic research and educational services.

The problems of plant bargaining could also be eased if trade unions were reorganised into more rational bargaining groups. One method of accomplishing this is through amalgamations. The TUC has repeatedly passed resolutions on the subject and launched comprehensive structural inquiries. And indeed there have been results. The number of trade unions declined from 1,384 in 1920 to 574 in 1966. Also membership is being concentrated in the largest organi-

[1] *Donovan Report, loc. cit.*, p. 188.

sations. Three members out of ten are affiliated to the three largest unions, the Transport and General Workers' Union, the Amalgamated Union of Engineers and Foundry Workers and the General and Municipal Workers' Union. Altogether 53 unions have been involved in mergers of one kind or another since 1964.

But the amalgamation process is not an easy one. It is only natural for trade unionists to resist a process which involves loss of identity and of autonomy for "their" union. This reluctance reflects much more than mere conservatism. It relates to such tangible problems as differentials between unions in scale of contributions and benefits; the disinclination of stronger unions to pool financial resources with weaker unions; conflicting policies with respect to organisation, wage demands, fringe benefits, etc.; and the problem of officials who might be made redundant by mergers. Craft unionists in particular are resistant to proposals for amalgamation with other occupations or reorganisation along industry lines.

Even where mergers do not prove practicable, however, it should be possible for unions to stop competing with each other on the plant floor. The Donovan Report suggests that:

> Apart from mergers, the most practical way to reduce multi-unionism is by agreements between unions on recruiting rights and negotiating rights. Where, for example, unions compete for membership among workers of the same grade in a single factory, as is not uncommon among non-craft workers in the engineering industry, it would be possible for the unions mainly concerned . . . to agree that in each factory only one of them would have the right to recruit among these grades in future. Subsequently existing members of the other unions might be persuaded to transfer to the union which has the recruitment rights, and these other unions would be able to give up their rights of representation. The success of the agreement would of course depend on matching losses and gains for each union. The principle is also capable of application on a wider basis. In instances where separate craft unions are not involved it could lead to a single union for manual workers in each factory. It could also be extended to transfers of rights within companies, to produce a single union for each grade of worker, or for all manual workers, throughout a multi-plant company. There are even cases, especially where the two great general unions are concerned, in which transfers of rights between industries might be achieved.[1]

---

[1] *Donovan Report, loc. cit.*, 182.

2. *Employer Associations*

One reform that will be required in the structure of employer organisations is changes designed to make it possible for employer members of such organisations to participate in productivity bargaining without finding themselves in contravention of association regulations, or even having to disaffiliate. The Donovan Report suggests that associations should "in the future . . . find their main purpose in the promotion of their members' interests by assisting them to develop orderly and efficient systems of industrial relations within their undertakings and by *confining common rules to those areas where they can be applied without hindering this development*". (Italics added.)[1]

At another point in the report this is spelled out in more detail.

> Accordingly there would be advantage in an agreement between the association and the unions which set out guidelines for acceptable company or factory agreements and exempted such agreements from the obligation to uphold all the terms of the existing industry-wide agreements.[2]

The Engineering Employers' Federation argues for a positive role for employer associations in regulating variations in earnings at plant level. It suggests that such regulations could be accomplished by:

> (i) Setting out agreed criteria in national agreements.
>
> (ii) Requiring local associations to examine and register plant agreements and in consultation with district officials of the trade unions who are parties not only to the plant bargains but to the national bargain, determine if the national criteria are observed.
>
> (iii) Permitting no variation in earnings (except approved effort bargains of the BBR type) other than accomplished by an agreement in which an increase in productivity can be established.
>
> (iv) Proposed productivity bargains which involve variations to national agreements in respect of *conditions* as opposed to rates will of course be picked up by local associations and the decision whether to allow these to be included could be subject to the approval of a standing sub-committee of the appropriate National Technical Committee before seeking joint agreement.
>
> (v) Using the knowledge and experience of local associations to assist member firms to set up equitable and effective productivity bargains

---

[1] *Ibid.*, p. 198.

[2] *Donovan Report, loc. cit.*, p. 44.

(and from their unrivalled knowledge of procedure, picking up snags which might otherwise result in resort to procedure).[1]

The Engineering Employers' Federation also proposes the appointment of National Technical Committees on a trade sectional basis to design meaningful industry guidelines to productivity bargaining. Under the guidance of the NTC's, local associations could assist member firms in their productivity bargaining by:

(a) Consultation with member firms on setting up objectives and notably in giving advice on the industrial relations implications of these objectives.

(b) Giving assistance during negotiations with shop stewards and district officials and in the drawing up of the final agreement; clearly an important responsibility in this connection would not only be to ensure that the proposed N.T.C. guidelines are observed but that the agreement does not conflict in principle with whatever national agreements apply.

(c) Registering agreements and assisting in follow up.

(d) Circulating members with information on the agreements, their success and/or difficulties experienced.[2]

Most employers' associations would, however, agree that, like trade unions, they need more full time officials with a higher degree of training and expertise, and that there is a strong case for amalgamations among smaller associations in order to ensure better services to members.

Of the 108 organisations in membership of the CBI, 75 combine the functions of an employers' association with that of a trade association, and 33 operate solely as employers' associations. The number of combined organisations has been growing. Single all-purpose associations have recently been formed in chemicals, in rubber manufacturing and in ship-building and ship-repairing. In chemicals and rubber the amalgamations were soon followed by the radical revision of their industry-wide agreements in a progressive direction. Combined organisations have advantages which others should carefully consider. The separation of industrial relations from commercial matters is an unreal dichotomy. It is easier for an employer to play a full and active part in the affairs of one association than to do so in two separate associations. Combined organisations are thus better able to draw on their members' experience and to profit from their suggestions, and can in turn exercise more influence over members' policies than would otherwise be possible. Economies in operating costs are also feasible.

---

[1] *Loc cit.*, p. 24.
[2] *Loc cit.*, p. 17.

> For these reasons the foundation in 1965 of the CBI to centralise in one national organisation the responsibility for dealing with the whole range of matters which affect employers was a considerable step forward. It is a further advantage that the experience of the nationalised industries in matters of industrial relations should be pooled with that of private industry, since so many of the problems in this field are common to both sections of industry. The CBI, in contrast with the previous British Employers' Confederation, admits individual companies into membership as well as employers' associations. Non-federated companies such as Ford and Vauxhall can therefore make a contribution to the work of the CBI.[1]

There is another basic requirement if national organisations of employers and of trade unions are to exercise real influence over workplace bargaining. This is the creation of adequate machinery and appropriate attitudes for *joint control* at the plant level. Joint control means effective worker participation in decision making. This issue, which is complex and controversial, is the subject matter of the next chapter.

### C. *National Bargaining for Minimum Standards : Plant Bargaining for Increases*

There is a third approach to two-tier bargaining which proposes that the role of national agreements should be restricted, leaving the bulk of negotiating over wages and conditions to productivity bargaining at the plant level. This is an approach that must be given careful attention since it appears to be the current position of both the NBPI and the Royal Commission on Trade Unions and Employers' Associations.

Summarising what it considers to be the arguments against national bargaining, the Board stated that a possible verdict could be that "the national agreement might therefore now be regarded as a redundant historical survival".[2] But it recoiled from writing off the traditional British system of collective bargaining in such a definitive manner, and quickly added:

> We consider, however, that there are many respects in which industry-wide negotiating and conciliation systems can serve a valuable purpose. In particular, apart from providing a desirable common framework of

---

[1] *Donovan Report, loc. cit.*, pp. 200–201.

[2] NBPI Report No. 65, *loc. cit.*, p. 59.

standard condition in such matters as working hours and holiday arrangements, they can be developed so as to provide external support and guidance for the reform of payment systems at the enterprise.[1]

It then presented an outline of this more restricted role for national bargaining as follows:

> If industry-wide agreements are to fulfil this role of helping to reform the system of payment at the enterprise, it seems to us that they must cease to concern themselves primarily with the negotiation of general "across the board" pay increases. They should, we think, rather aim to meet four main functions. First, to promote the conclusion of plant or company agreements by, for instance, negotiating standard procedures for bargaining at the enterprise level. Secondly, to lay down general guidelines for plant payment systems, allowing for variations in local or sectional conditions as far as possible. Thirdly, to provide a means of correcting faults in such systems as they arise. And fourthly, to correct adverse consequences of plant wage-determination by *selective* wage increases to groups such as the low-paid or others whose pay needs to be changed in relation to the rest of the industry. If, for example, increases in earnings at the plant level can be kept below the average rate of increase in national productivity, scope is left for doing something for the low-paid through a national agreement without incurring inflation.[2]

The Royal Commission is similarly forthright in stating that:

> The overriding need is to put an end to the conflict between the pretence of industry-wide agreements and the realities of industrial relations. Industry-wide agreements are capable of dealing with the length of the standard working week and the length of the annual holidays. Most industry-wide agreements on pay, however, cannot effectively settle more than minimum rates and their periodic adjustment. *What they can all do is to set out what matters companies are expected to settle for themselves and provide guidance on how it should be done.*[3]
>
> Accordingly there would be advantage in an agreement between the association and the unions which set out guide-lines for acceptable company or factory agreements and exempted such agreements from the obligation to uphold all the terms of the existing industry-wide agreement. . . .
>
> Agreements to raise minimum rates of pay are no more to be preferred than others, for the general practice is that, each time the minimum is raised, the pay of all workers covered by the agreement is raised by the same amount regardless of whether existing pay exceeds the minimum and by how much. This objection to industry-wide pay

---

[1] *Ibid.*
[2] *Donovan Report, loc. cit.*, p. 59.
[3] *Ibid.*, p. 43.

> agreements can be removed by negotiating minimum earnings levels for a standard working week. Companies within the association can then negotiate productivity agreements confident that, so long as their employees' earnings for the standard week are in excess of the prescribed minimum level set out in any subsequent industry-wide agreement, they would not be obliged to raise their pay again. It would also enable industry-wide agreements to set more realistic levels of minimum pay without causing all-round inflation in costs.[1]

In short, it is being proposed that:

—collective bargaining should be conducted primarily at the local level through plant productivity agreements; and that

—national agreements should no longer establish across-the-board increases in standard rates;

—but should be limited to;

(a) advising firms on productivity bargaining at the local level;

(b) supervising the resulting wage structure and correcting resulting anomalies; and

(c) negotiating selective wage increases for lower-paid workers.

In assessing this approach, it is important to note that it is *not* a straightforward proposal to scrap national bargaining and replace it with plant bargaining. If it were, it could not logically be discussed in a section on "two-tier" bargaining. Moreover, it could then be evaluated in terms of a critique of the American system, which is almost entirely a plant bargaining system.

> Plant bargaining on the American model is not supplementary to national bargaining but alternative to it, and if it became widespread in Britain it would, if that pattern were followed, be a substitute for it. That the extent of plant bargaining might undermine the well established British system of collective bargaining is not an argument in itself. But it must be recognised that plant bargaining and productivity bargaining must be looked at in this wider context.[2]

But the most significant feature of this NBPI-Royal Commission proposal is that it does *not* put exclusive stress on plant bargaining.

---

[1] *Ibid.*, pp. 44–45.
[2] TUC, *op. cit.*

On the contrary, it is quite specific about the functions to be performed by national industrywide negotiations. At the same time—and this is the crux of the matter—its tone suggests that these are marginal or peripheral functions designed merely to support a system of plant bargaining.

In fact, however, the issues which are so blithely assigned to national negotiators are the basic problems,

—which have always bedevilled British industrial relations;

—which have been the main target of most of the work of the Board and of the Royal Commission in this field;

—and which largely determine the effectiveness of a system of collective bargaining. And yet no guidance is offered as to just how the problem should be tackled at the national level. It seems rather to be a matter of wistfully wishing them away from the local scene where they only complicate the otherwise logical and compelling arguments for plant productivity bargaining.

There are many problems in the fields of industrial relations and of productive efficiency to which plant bargaining can make a significant contribution. At the same time, and at the risk of repetition, it must be stressed that plant bargaining undermines solidarity and the concept of the "rate for the job". It can be useful in the effort to bring order and coherence into the pay structure *within a plant or enterprise*. But because of its effect on pay differentials, it exacerbates the difficulties of achieving a rational wage structure *within an industry and throughout the economy*.

This is not an argument against productivity bargaining. But it does throw into bold relief the central issues involved in collective bargaining—and indeed in an incomes policy. And it emphasises the importance of a two-tier bargaining structure in which the *major*—not the *minor*—responsibility rests upon the national organisations on both sides and on the ways in which they can bring their influences to bear on bargaining at plant level as well as in national negotiations.

It is worth outlining the kind of responsibility which the proposal would thrust upon national negotiations—and on which it has offered no guidance at all. Not that the missing blue prints can be supplied here. Not even a new Royal Commission and another five years of exhaustive investigation could achieve the insight, the negotiating machinery, the good will and the expertise in working together that will be required by employer associations and trade unions if genuine productivity bargaining at plant level is to be meshed into an overall framework of negotiations at the national level to achieve a rational and equitable wage structure consonant with an effective prices and incomes policy. But at least some hint can be given of the kind of problems involved.

The proposal that nationally negotiated increases should be transformed from standard rates into realistic minimum rates with increases above this minimum being negotiated at local level represents a fundamental change. As matters now stand, nationally negotiated rates are the platform on which additional payments are made. Thus increases in national rates affect all workers, not just those receiving the basic rate. In short, increases in national rates mean general increases throughout the industry. But if national rates were declared to be minimum rates, they would result in increases only for those workers whose earnings were currently below the new minimum.

If national negotiators were at the same time given responsibility for correcting anomalies in pay structure resulting from increases granted at the local level, this would give rise to a difficult problem of *allocation*. The presumption is that a portion of the overall increase in productivity for the industry would be "reserved" for this purpose, rather than being completely absorbed by increases at the local level. But what mechanism is envisaged for keeping plant wage increases below average productivity in order to provide such a margin? And *who* would allocate the margin as between industries and according to what formula?

The *enforcement* problem would be even more difficult than that of allocation. Local plant agreements would have to be carefully policed to ensure that they were consonant with national guidelines, that they corresponded to genuine productivity increases, and to prevent leapfrogging and whipsawing. This is an enormous task far beyond the existing resources or authority of local employer associations or trade officers. It is difficult to see what sanctions would be available, or how the problem of multi-unionism could be overcome. The proposal seems to assume a degree of centralisation in collective bargaining which is so far quite remote in Britain.

There are, to be sure, a few indications that trade unions are tentatively moving in this direction. These include the continuing process of union amalgamation; the TUC's evolving wage vetting procedure; and a growing interest in synchronising wage claims. The TUC *Economic Review* for 1968 puts the case for supplementing the notification system by a procedure under which the TUC General Council

> would discuss with all the unions concerned, if possible at the same time or at least during a limited period, the submission of the most important pattern-setting claims. This does not imply that claims would be submitted on a standardised basis, but it would give the unions an opportunity to determine collectively what their broad strategy should be for the following year (or years), whether in terms of the priority to be accorded to improvements in wages and hours and in other conditions and types of benefit, or in terms of the relative treatment of different groups of workers. In this way it should be possible to judge more accurately than is possible through the present system the merits of one course of action as against another, and it would also enable unions to participate more actively in the development of a positive incomes policy. . . . If agreement is reached that such a development would be desirable and practicable, the General Council should be in a position to put to the 1969 Conference of Executives their proposals for holding synchronised discussions in the autumn of 1969 about claims which would be submitted simultaneously in the spring of 1970.[1]

So far, however, the TUC has not gotten beyond internal and informal consideration of these proposals. Also it appears that it will move cautiously, and will concentrate first on co-ordination by workers in allied fields such as engineering and metal; professional and scientific workers; woodworkers and furniture trades—and perhaps unions, such as those in local government, which already cooperate in submitting separate but similar claims. But first the leaders of these individual unions must be persuaded that they would not thereby be surrendering their authority.

---

[1] *Economic Review, loc. cit.*, p. 67.

## Summary

Of the 14 million workers covered by voluntary national negotiating machinery, almost half are also covered by local or company bargaining. But the influence of informal local bargaining is more widespread than indicated by these figures because of the pervasive influence of factory bargaining on earnings in wage council industries and in public services, and because of high earnings' supplements at local level.

*National bargaining* is basic to the traditional British system of collective bargaining. Employers like it because it precludes competitive wage cutting and the process of "whipsawing"; pools their individual bargaining strengths; economises on bargaining effort; and provides a national framework for regulating the wage structure. Above all, they like its flexibility which permits of informal bargaining at local level without contractual commitment. And trade unions like national bargaining for many of the same reasons, that is, it protects them against competitive wage cutting, provides national standards for wage structure, pools their bargaining strengths, imposes less strain on negotiators and permits additional increases at the local level. Both sides admit, however, that national bargaining has failed to achieve solidarity or rationality in the wage structure, and that it has contributed to wage drift and inflation.

Meanwhile there has been a marked shift to wage determination at *local level*. This is largely because enterprises are too diverse to permit of industry-wide standardisation except in relation to a few key minimum rates and general guidelines on differentials, hours and fringe benefits. Because most vital issues have to be determined at plant level, national bargains have been supplemented by workshop agreements which are not necessarily in conflict with them. Employer associations have acquiesced in this development because they are impotent to do otherwise, and because they don't want the responsibility involved in national regulation of earnings; however, many of them do worry about the effect on their influence and authority. Similarly, trade unions admit the necessity of local bargaining, but worry about its effect on trade union "grip" over their members.

Thus there are good reasons for factory bargaining. But at the same time, many of the issues which arise at plant level have implications which cut across industry. This makes it imperative for general principles to be established at a higher level in order to:

—safeguard the strength of trade unions and employers' associations which results from pooling of bargaining power,

—protect solidarity and standardisation of wage rates and conditions, and

—alleviate the fear of whipsawing and pressure on marginal firms.

In short, there is a need for two-tier bargaining in which agreements reached in the workshop are articulated with, and incorporated into, formal collective agreements at a high level.

At least three different approaches to two-tier bargaining have been suggested.

1. Broad guidelines for and general supervision of productivity bargaining in an industry could be provided by agreement *at the national level* and the actual agreements would be reached at the local level within the guidelines laid down nationally. Such a development would have far-reaching implications in terms of managerial prerogative and of rationalisation of the wage structure throughout industry.

2. Both trade unions and employers' associations could be given more leverage *at plant level* through productivity bargains which remove basic issues from unilateral managerial discretion and bring them into the framework of formal collective bargaining. But to be effective this would require drastic changes in trade unions (a more rational union structure, integrating shop stewards more closely with the unions, and providing more training, information and services) and in employers' associations (revised structure, better training, and providing industry guidelines for productivity bargaining).

3. The third proposal would, like the first proposal, leave the bulk of negotiations over wages and conditions to productivity bargaining at the plant level but it would assign to national agree-

ments the crucial tasks of advising firms on productivity bargaining, supervising the resulting wage structure, correcting anomalies resulting from it and negotiating selective wage increases for lower-paid workers. However, proponents of this approach have not explained how national negotiators could solve the enormous problems of allocation and of enforcement in correcting anomalies in pay structure. Indeed, the far-reaching implications of this proposal have so far not been acknowledged.

Chapter VIII

# Productivity Bargaining and Worker Participation

## Implications of Industrial Change

"The growing complexity of today's technological society makes the case for industrial democracy stronger and more urgent than ever in the past."

This statement from the paper presented to the 1968 Labour Conference by its National Executive Committee is the key point of this chapter.

For the politician, today's problems are always more urgent than any that preceded them. Yet there is evidence from a number of other countries, as well as the United Kingdom, that pressures for effective worker participation are mounting. The subject has been very much "in the air" recently in France, Germany, Norway, the Netherlands, Sweden and Italy. And even in the Socialist countries where worker control has been nominally in operation for many years, current economic developments in the direction of decentralisation appear to be giving it new meaning and effectiveness.

The source of these pressures has been fully documented in preceding pages. Sharper competition and rising costs are forcing employers to strive for greater marginal efficiency, particularly in the field of manpower utilisation. To achieve this they must have the cooperation of workers. But workers are conscious of growing threats to their jobs, their incomes, their status and their security as a result of economic concentration and technological innovation. Hence they will agree to change only to the extent that they are assured of protection from its adverse effects and of a fair share in its benefits. Such assurances, however, can in their view only be guaranteed if they themselves participate in making the relevant decisions.

Again in the words of the National Executive of the Labour Party:

> An extension of industrial democracy, and the effective participation of workers in decision making in individual industries and firms is therefore urgent and essential if the nation is to meet the human needs of those confronted by the major structural changes that are now taking place.

## The Concept of Managerial Prerogative

Views on industrial democracy are very much coloured by the concept of "managerial prerogative". And this concept underlies the attitudes of many more people than would admit it—or, indeed, who would realise that they are influenced by it.

On the surface the idea of "managerial prerogative" is eminently reasonable. Essentially it emphasises that *the owners* of a business have the right—indeed, the responsibility—of managing it, or of delegating that responsibility to managers accountable solely to them. This right is exercised by virtue of their ownership of the business. Any breaches of the principle—through extension of decision-making authority to other parties—are to be made unilaterally and voluntarily at the discretion of the owner-managers.

Collective agreements on wages and working conditions represent such a voluntary abrogation of managerial prerogative. On the other hand, managers have tended to retain their prerogative to decide unilaterally on such issues as distribution of overtime, hiring and firing of workers, manning of machines, pace of work, introduction of new machinery and new jobs, etc. As the Donovan Report has pointed out, this means that:

> These matters have therefore usually been excluded from formal negotiations, and—piecework apart—decisions on pay have been largely divorced from decisions about the work which is to be done for the pay; this being within managerial prerogative. Accordingly, where arrangements have been made with workers and shop stewards on methods of work, they have also tended to be informal.[1]

---

[1] *Loc. cit.*, p. 25.

The link between ownership and right to manage may strike the observer as obvious and incontrovertible. And yet one of the most widely commented-on economic phenomena of recent years has been the divorce between shareholders and management of private enterprise. Most shareholders simply do not bother to exercise their right of control. Others give theirs away via proxy voting. And the process of by-passing—or as Galbraith says, "disenfranchising"—shareholders is completed by concentrating really vital decisions in the hands of Boards of Directors.

It may be argued that this development does nothing to alter the principle of ownership as the source of the right to manage. It merely reflects the *delegation* of that right to a body of professional managers who make decisions on behalf of shareholders. The delegation of authority is, after all, an increasingly common characteristic of modern democracy.

But there is growing doubt as to whether modern management actually does reach decisions exclusively, or even primarily, in the light of the interests of shareholders—that is, with the object of maximising profit. Leading entrepreneurs are the first to acknowledge that they have responsibility also to many interests other than shareholders—to consumers, to employees whose lives are shaped by their jobs, to the government whose protection and assistance is vital to their viability, and to the internal and external soundness of the economy.

These responsibilities are more than academic. Tangible evidence of their significance can be found in the extent to which managerial prerogative is limited by external intervention. Management discretion is severely circumscribed by government decree, by organised action on the part of consumers, by the will of semi-autonomous work groups within the enterprise, and by collective agreements with trade unions.

There are many ways in which the State intervenes in private enterprise. Managerial prerogative is restricted by legislation against monopoly, by requirements under company law, by zoning regulations, by legislation prohibiting false weights and measures or discrimination in employment; by manpower regulations concerning protection of women workers or young workers or night workers or safety or hygiene in the plant or location of industry, and in many other ways. In effect the State rules that there are interests involved which have a prior claim over those of shareholders; namely, the interests of consumers, or of workers, or of the "general public".

Similarly, we have seen that groups of workers within an enterprise exercise a kind of autonomous control over managerial decisions in order to protect their own interests and aspirations. They do this in many ways, all of them informal and unauthorised, and without benefit of institutional machinery. These include temporary "coalitions" of workers, *ad hoc* petition committees, concerted action by strike leaders, social pressures or sanctions, informal agreements or undertakings between shop stewards and supervisors and various restrictive practices of the kind described in Chapter III.

When managerial intervention by workers reaches the stage of negotiation between trade unions and representatives of employers, it is written into a collective agreement. In their early days, trade unions were considered by many to be a serious encroachment on the rights of management. In the end this kind of intervention was "accepted" by employers only when they found they could no longer resist it. In this case, as with informal work group sanctions, employers relinquish a portion of their managerial prerogative, reluctantly and only because they are forced to.

For their part, workers base their claim to participate in managerial decisions on the degree of their personal stake in the enterprise. This is parallel to the logic of State intervention to protect interests of higher priority than those of shareholders. The underlying assumption appears to be that the right to manage is related to the degree of involvement. Ownership is only one kind of interest in an enterprise and usually not the most significant.

The lives of workers are largely shaped by the employment situation in the firm, and work people feel that they should have an effective voice in determining their own destinies. They think they are entitled to participate in vital decisions at plant or company level concerning not only the pay for work, but also the work to be done for the pay.

> When we talk about worker participation we mean that within a factory or place of work those who invest their lives in the business by working for their employer, whether it be a public employer or a private employer, should have a definite say as to the way in which the job is done—the whole job.[1]

There is no doubt, therefore, that workers have a very direct and immediate interest in managerial decisions because these have an important impact on their lives. *But does this interest entitle them to claim the right of co-decision?*

This is the basic issue. Before tackling it, it might be helpful to be clear as to the nature of the managerial function. Is "management" a distinct profession sharply differentiated from the productive process? Does it require specialised skills and knowledge unrelated to those involved in production?

Certainly the management *function* is distinct from other productive functions. It is essentially a job of *coordination.* A manager must take an overall view of the flow of work under his jurisdiction. It is his responsibility to ensure that the efforts of individuals and the results of separate processes are meshed in such a way that the right output merges at the right time in the right place in the right quality and quantity.

It is not helpful, however, to think of the management function as occurring at one or even a few particular centres of the enterprise separate from the production flow, like the podium of the orchestra conductor. Nor can the dynamics of the management function be found in a few key decisions made centrally and independently of workers.

*On the contrary, managerial decisions are being made constantly at all levels of operation and right through the productive process.* All managers are employees. And any employee who makes a decision that will affect the tempo, or flow, or quality or quantity of output is in a sense exercising a managerial function.

To some this may appear to be carrying matters too far to the point of *reducto ad absurdum.* Logically, however, there is no

---

[1] Jack Jones, Transport and General Workers Union, in an interview reported in *Sunday Times,* 2 June 1968.

earlier stopping point once the diffuseness of the managerial function is acknowledged.

Supervisors are obviously "managers" in so far as they give instructions and make choices between alternative production methods or materials or manning charts or time schedules. But this means that foremen are also "managers". And so are craftsmen who give instructions to their mates, or plan their own work. And so are shop stewards who transmit, or dispute, the decisions of foremen.

Professional, technical, scientific and administrative workers and experts of all kinds are "managers" because they make production decisions based on the results of their experiments or technical knowledge; and issue instructions and listen to the views of their assistants and other subordinates and report these to those higher in the hierarchy. And the leaders of (formal or informal) work groups are also "managers" for the same reasons.

Board members make decisions based partly on decisions made by department heads based partly on decisions made by middle management based partly on decisions made by "first-line" management based partly on decisions made by leaders of work groups based partly on decisions made by workers of all kinds including unskilled manual labourers.

The point has been belaboured in order to underline the significance of "devolution of responsibility" for management. In this context the word "devolution" is more expressive than "decentralisation" because it emphasises that many key decisions (for example, on investment, purchasing,, introduction of new methods and machinery) are made centrally at top level—even though they reflect the views and expertise and decisions of employees all along the line.

The principle of devolution of responsibility has a bearing on managerial prerogative. It suggests that the right to make managerial decisions derives from a combination of *competence and degree of interest*. Whenever there is a choice at any level—on manning, methods, machinery, material, timing, equipment, pay or whatever—the decision should be made by those most knowledgeable and most immediately concerned.

Admittedly such an interpretation of managerial prerogative invites problems arising from conflicts of interest. But this merely demonstrates that the interpretation is realistic. Industrial relations are necessarily a reflection of a power struggle between conflicting interests, and they will never be understood, much less ameliorated, unless approached from this premise.

The interested parties in any private enterprise include *inter alia* the employees from manual labourers to top executives, members of the Board of Directors, shareholders, suppliers, customers and the Government. The various objectives of these parties include jobs (level and security); income from employment; profits; status, prestige, power (authority); and productivity (efficiency). And the degree of interest of each party varies, from that of the worker who has no other source of income and perhaps of meaningfulness in life to the wealthy individual whose vast investment portfolio includes a few shares of the company's stocks.

Most of the employees of the firm, including the executives, have a very direct interest in the content of their jobs and the level and security of income from them, and in the relative status and authority they provide. To the extent that they compete with each other in these respects, there can be conflicts of interest.

The level of profits is of direct concern to shareholders and to Boards of Directors, and also to executives in so far as their performance, and hence career and income, is judged by profitability. The quest for higher profits often conflicts with workers' interests in higher wages.

Finally, productivity is of direct concern to shareholders because of its influence on profits. It also has an important bearing on the career prospects, prestige and incomes of executives at various levels. But worker interest in productivity depends upon the extent to which the level and the stability of their earnings are related to productivity. One important effect of productivity bargaining has been to give workers a more direct stake in the efficiency of the work operation by relating their incomes to productivity. And precisely because productivity bargaining increases their degree of interest in productivity, it by the same token enhances workers' right to participate in the way the work is organised and paid for, especially since there is no question of their competence in terms of familiarity with the job to be done.

## Consultation versus Negotiation

During World War II a number of "joint consultative committees" were established at plant level. They were not supposed to deal with matters normally covered by existing collective agreements, but productivity and increased efficiency were considered suitable subjects for discussion. After the war it was decided to continue these committees in operation; also the new nationalised industries established similar committees. In most private firms the representatives are elected by workers, and in nationalised industries by trade unions. These committees are purely advisory. Items settled by collective bargaining are explicitly excluded from consideration.

These joint bodies usually have a very general mandate for "promoting sound relations in the undertaking", "general improvement of productivity", "better communication and workplace information", or "to obtain the views of employees in order to avoid misunderstandings". Such vague terms of reference are obviously open to wide interpretation. On the other hand, since they do not provide for co-decision, there is no need to be specific.

The system was based on the notion that joint consultation is appropriate only where employee and employer interests coincide. Other issues involving a conflict of interests were to be settled by collective bargaining negotiations.

Experience has proved the fallacy of the assumption that there are issues of such common interest to both workers and employers that negotiations are not required. It is clear that joint consultative committees cannot survive unless they become negotiating committees. Otherwise they are boycotted by shop stewards who have no use for committees which cannot reach decisions, or impose sanctions, or appeal to trade union solidarity. Nor are workers or trade unions inclined to accept the notion that there are areas of management activity, such as introduction of new machinery, level of output and methods of work arrangement, which are the exclusive prerogative of management, merely to be discussed with and explained to workers' representatives so that interests will "converge". They believe that any subject which affects their work is a fit and proper matter for negotiation.

Thus it appears that the system of consultation as it has developed in Britain can only retain a role in the workplace system of labour relations where unionisation and shop steward representation are weak or non-existent.

Until recently consultation and negotiation tended to be two distinct processes.

Consultation has taken place primarily at plant level through formally established joint bodies consisting of representatives of management and of workers in the shop; only very occasionally were these latter appointed as official trade union representatives. In so far as consultation or negotiations occurred informally at plant level with shop stewards, it still did not constitute a link in the chain of collective bargaining, since shop stewards are not usually formally recognised by employers as accredited union spokesmen for workers in the shop, and their negotiating functions are not defined in union rules.

Meetings of joint consultative committees were scheduled regularly. Discussions were specifically limited to matters not normally the subject of negotiations. The scope of the discussions was restricted to the particular factory or workshop unit without reference to other levels of activity. And the final decision on issues discussed rested with management.

*Negotiation,* on the other hand, has occurred primarily at regional or national level between representatives of employers' associations and full-time trade union officials. In so far as negotiations took place at plant level between management and shop stewards, it was informal, usually unwritten, and did not represent a firm irrevocable commitment by the employers. These negotiations were arranged not regularly but *ad hoc* as the occasion arose. Discussions were generally restricted to a few major issues like increases in standard wage rates, hours, and holidays. The scope of the negotiations was industry-wide. And the final decision was arrived at *jointly* as a compromise between the claims of management and of workers.

**Productivity Bargaining Formalises Worker Participation**

Productivity bargaining has the effect of bringing trade unions into the workshop and thereby fusing consultation and negotiation into one process. It formalises practices which have hitherto been informally agreed or at least accepted by workers through their shop stewards. In this way it gives the workers greater control. If real power is to be conferred, it must necessarily be spelled out in detail.

Prior to the advent of productivity bargaining there were very few formal collective agreements negotiated at plant level—and few specific rules or procedures governing relations between shop stewards and employees. Agreements were arrived at orally, usually in short *ad hoc* shop floor meetings during a break, and they were seldom recorded in written documents. These informal understandings usually covered vital issues not dealt with in collective agreements negotiated at national or regional level. These include lieu rates, piecework prices, bonuses, plus payments, job descriptions, work loads, overtime, introduction of new machinery, job evaluation, conditions, hours, discipline, grievances, manning, redundancy, job allocation, supplies, promotion, grading, tools and job specifications.

But productivity bargaining has changed this pattern. To obtain the assent of workers to changes in work organisation, pay structure and methods of production, it has been found necessary to conclude formal, explicit agreements with trade union officials at plant level and to establish joint machinery for negotiation and administration of the agreements.

Productivity agreements involve full recognition of trade unions as the voice of workers in the plant. And they extend the subject area of formal collective bargaining by removing vital issues concerned with industrial change from unilateral decision making by employers or by work groups and bringing them into the framework of joint negotiation and regulation. This reduces the element of arbitrariness in managerial decisions and makes them more predictable, more reliable and more enforceable.

Thus productivity bargaining goes a long way towards meeting the demands in the statement presented to the Labour Party by its National Executive:

> that the development of industrial democracy should be pursued through the creation of a *single channel* of communication between workers' representatives and management. The scope and subject matter of collective bargaining should be extended so that all the elements of management (dismissals, discipline, introduction of new machinery, forward planning of manpower, rationalisation and so forth) are within the sphere of *negotiations* at plant and national level.

Trade unionists are clearly influenced in their thinking by the principle of devolution of responsibility. For them this principle means that workers should participate in management through their various representatives at every appropriate level. The "appropriate" level is the level at which the relevant decisions are taken. And "participation" should take place in discussion units commensurate with the range of effects produced by technological change. Participation increases acceptability of change, but it also involves the acceptance of responsibility.

Thus in its evidence to the Royal Commission on Trade Unions and Employers' Associations the TUC asked for:

> Whatever is the normal body which regularly meets at plant level to take decisions on the running of that plant.
>
> Trade union representation at intermediate levels, for example, at regional level or at a level which represents the functional authority for the particular product within the enterprise.
>
> At top level, legislation to allow companies, if they wish, to make provision for trade union representation on boards of directors.

It is self-evident that productivity bargaining emphasises trade union responsibility at the plant level. Most productivity agreements have been concluded with individual employers and have regulated relationships at the plant level. At the same time, the contribution of productivity bargaining to trade union authority at the level of the industry should not be under-rated. In some instances productivity agreements have covered all plants in the industry. More important, however, is the effect which company or plant productivity agreements have in emphasising certain major issues which must be resolved by trade unions and national employer organisations at a higher level. As noted earlier, the negotiation of plant agreements and the development of guidelines for productivity bargains has forced the parties involved, as well as the Government (through the National Board for Prices and Incomes) and such independent bodies as the Royal Commission—to face up explicitly to the wider implications of plant bargaining for differentials, income distribution and incomes policy. Also it has become clear that certain forms of worker protection will have increasingly to be provided at a higher level than the workshop—for example, minimum wages, regulation of dismissals, redundancy and training benefits, and protection in cases of job transfer.

There are many, including some trade unionists, who argue against formal worker participation in managerial decisions on grounds of "divided loyalty". They point out that trade unions are external to the firm and can limit the freedom of an enterprise and its workers to determine the terms of employment. It is the function of this external organisation to defend workers' interests as opposed to those of management. This it can hardly do effectively while at the same time participating in managerial decisions. The trade union role of "opposition" cannot be carried out by sitting "on both sides of the table". It is not up to the trade unions to do the employer's job for him, and any attempt to do so would compromise their independence. Trade unions must retain their militancy and not allow themselves to be associated with maximisation of profits, the wastes of destructive competition or monopolistic exploitation of consumers.

Although a few individual trade unionists still retain this reluctance to accept managerial responsibilities, the TUC has shifted a long way from this position. In its evidence to the Royal Commission the TUC stated:

> The earlier rigidity of union views on non-participation in management were . . . based on false abstractions and do not even correspond to present-day workshop reality. . . . To say that trade unions cannot limit or control management if they become part of it is to play with words. If management is defined as the function of seeing that the work gets out at the other end at the right time, work peoples' representatives are already part of the substance of management, and it would be a considerable step forward if this role were more explicitly recognised.[1]

---

[1] *Loc. cit.*, p. 103.

Since the trade union objective is to limit the unilateral exercise of responsibility by managers, it follows that they must be prepared themselves to accept responsibility. The managerial function devolves upon all those involved in the production process. All managers are employees and all employees are managers. They cannot expect to opt out of this responsibility.

Every forward step in the direction of industrial democracy involves the assumption of responsibility. This is obviously true in the case of collective agreements above the plant level.

> Any process of collective bargaining sets limits to the freedom of action of the participants, since they are called on to respect the agreements they have entered into. But this is not an encroachment on union 'independence' so long as the right to withdraw from agreements is maintained. If there is a failure to agree there is no joint responsibility for managerial action.[1]

Responsibility limits independence, but does not contravene it so long as there is still a right to withdraw and to negotiate.

Many employers on the other hand still resist the process of formalising trade union participation in plant negotiations. They dislike transforming *de facto* rights into *de jure* rights which cannot be withdrawn and hence constitute a precedent. They are not anxious to strengthen trade unions by increasing their authority and prestige. They argue that workers' representatives don't have the necessary expertise for making managerial decisions and that not all shop stewards are reliable. Above all they are hesitant to explicitly acknowledge the erosion of managerial prerogative.

## Continuous Participation

Productivity bargaining implies a continuing process of participation at plant level. "Participation" is a blend of consultation and negotiation on a regular basis through formally instituted machinery which is fully integrated into the framework of collective bargaining and fully backed by the sanctions and the services available to each side from local, regional and national organisations external to the plant.

---

[1] *Industrial Democracy,* Working Party Report, The Labour Party, June 1967, p. 22.

There has been a trend over a number of years for amalgamation of the two processes as consultation has been shifted into the area of conflicting interests and thus brought into the direct union–management relationship. Examples are ICI, Vauxhall, Glacier Metal Corporation, the Post Office and Electricity Supply.

In the last two or three years this trend has been dramatically accentuated by productivity bargaining. This is because successful negotiation and implementation of a productivity agreement require that changes originating at the plant or company level should be exhaustively investigated and discussed by management and trade unions and eventually agreed and then supervised by both sides. Moreover, once the concept of productivity bargaining is established at a plant, the process of bargaining is likely to be a continuing one. Productivity bargaining is a process of continuous adaptation of working practices to technological changes.

The NBPI has proposed that machinery should be set up at plant level for such on-going discussions.

> We do not believe that it is possible to exaggerate the importance of full discussion and agreement at plant and workshop level. Methods of work and industrial practices cannot be changed by decision of an individual or a company, but only by the men who do the work. Where there exists no formal machinery for plant or workshop negotiations, it should be created.[1]

And this is what is happening in a growing number of firms. As a result, the *same* issues are being discussed and decided by the *same* people through the *same* channel of participation. This is in contrast to the earlier situation where one set of workers and management people discussed, but did not decide, a prescribed set of issues in a joint consultative committee, while other issues were negotiated and agreed collectively by different people at a different level external to the plant.

But even though participation, once established on a continuing basis, would involve the same issues, the same people and the same institutional machinery, it would nevertheless embrace two distinct *phases* of discussion. For most issues and most of the time, dis-

---

[1] NBPI Report No. 36, *loc. cit.*, p. 38.

cussion would stop short of actual negotiation culminating in written agreements. At this stage it would involve a continuous examination procedure in which workers' representatives receive and supply information, act as a sounding board for management proposals, and express their views and make their own suggestions. In this way many changes could be instituted on a mutually satisfactory basis without their ever becoming issues of contention. Rumours could be scotched and uncertainty dispelled at the earliest possible moment. And workers would feel that they were having a real influence on managerial decisions.

> Generally speaking our industrial relations are almost unbelievably bad. . . . There are millions in industry who get no encouragement to use their brains or exert their interests outside the narrow confines of their individual jobs. Any group of workers that you care to ask—in a car factory, on a building site, in an office—will tell you that they can see ways in which materials, time and effort could be put to better use in the industry in which they work. Generally though it is nobody's job to get their views; certainly not the job of anybody who can break through the barriers of status and habit which sanctify too many wasteful practices in industry.
>
> Workers have in general had enough exhortations. What they need is effective machinery for putting forward their views and criticisms on the things that they see every day at work. . . . For managerial decisions to be subjected to the fire of comment from the men who see how they work would mean that in the end the decisions would be better ones. A man who has been convinced that the decisions which he is expected to observe are sensible and is further given the opportunity to contribute to those decisions is likely to be more productive than one who imagines that he is surrounded by waste and incomprehensible policies.[1]

This phase of participation is crucially dependent on adequate communication—communication between workers and their representatives, between workers' representatives and trade union officials, and between all levels of management. Effective communication in turn requires a complete and objective flow of information in both directions. As matters now stand, workers and trade unions are not inclined to trust much of the information supplied by employers. They are asking for more details on: man-

---

[1] *The Times,* 15 January 1968, article by Lord Delacourt-Smith, General Secretary of the Post Office Engineering Union.

power plans, wages and salaries, management salaries and fees, labour turnover, training proposals, labour costs per units of output, purchasing, distribution, selling and administrative costs; order books, production and investment plans, financial structure of the firm, directors's shareholding and internal management structure.

The statement on Industrial Democracy by the National Executive of the Labour Party argues that the right to more detailed information on a continuing basis should be ensured in a reform of company law, and that "it might even require that a company should in future present an annual report to its workers as well as to its shareholders, giving the required categories of information in general and intelligible terms".

Trade unionists also suggest that there should be investigation into areas in which workers might assume unilateral executive responsibility under the terms of a bargaining agreement. This might be possible for administration of welfare funds, regulation of overtime and even some aspects of selection and promotion.

The second phase of continuous participation at plant level would occur whenever there emerged certain areas of fundamental conflict over major issues of pay, conditions or job control which could not be resolved through active consultation between management and representatives of the workers in the particular shop. At this point the participants would agree to disagree, and the issues would pass into the stage of negotiation through external collective bargaining machinery. This right to withdraw into the area of compromise enables workers' representatives to retain their independence. This, indeed, is the basic answer to the charge that worker participation must involve divided loyalty.

We have already seen how important it is that an integral link should be established between vital issues which arise at the plant level and collective bargaining at the national level where major problems of wage structure and income distribution must ultimately be threshed out. Fragmented and informal workplace bargaining must be replaced by open negotiations between representative bodies at the operative level at which important issues emerge.

This operative level will be the level at which uniformity of control can be secured without negotiators losing touch with conditions and views in the workshop. This may be the plant, the enterprise, the regional or the national level. Whatever the level, agreements must be *explicit*. They must replace informal and uncoordinated workbench "undertakings" between workers and foremen reached not through open examination but rather on the basis of "custom and practice". Managerial decisions will never be coherent, effective and predictable as long as they are subject to dispersed, uncontrolled and obscure bargaining procedures. Nor will workers' representatives develop specialised knowledge and expertise on managerial functions and industrial relations until they are forced through continuous participation in decision-making to become part of a permanent dialogue between management and employees.

### Diversion on Profit-sharing

In Britain discussion of worker participation is usually restricted to participation in control of the enterprise. Worker participation in enterprise earnings, that is, profit-sharing, is usually dismissed as irrelevant or impractical or undesirable. Trade union and Labour Party spokesmen, particularly, have been prone to argue that industrial democracy should be based on the employee as a worker, not as an owner or "capitalist" profit-recipient. Workers prefer that unions should use their bargaining power to increase wages rather than to demand a share of profits.

This argument is reinforced by the point made earlier that the voting rights of shareholders do not exercise much influence over management. This would certainly be true for the small proportion of total shares that would in any event be held by any one worker.

There is also an understandable suspicion on the part of workers and trade unions of any kind of profit-sharing that would tie the proceeds to investment in the employing firm, or require it to be held in trust for the worker until a later date, for example upon retirement. This is usually rejected on the grounds that it reflects the kind of paternalism designed to "buy" the loyalty of workers and bind them to the firm, thereby restricting their mobility.

Moreover, it can be argued that profit-sharing of a more general kind, for example schemes for limiting the amount of profits to be paid to shareholders or re-invested in the firm and for distributing the surplus to workers in cash or transferable securities—would not necessarily have the desired incentive effect. Experience has shown that it is not much of a spur to workers to be told that "we'll all earn more if we all produce more". The more general the scope of the scheme and the more remote the decision—by "them"—as to how surplus is to be shared, the less the incentive effect is likely to be. It is pertinent to point out that in Socialist regimes where all workers are owners of all enterprise, few are actively concerned with productive efficiency.

It seems that workers are not really interested in level of efficiency or in participating in management unless these can be shown to have a tangible effect on their earnings. Why, they ask, should they make an effort to increase profits which will accrue to shareholders? Again this can be demonstrated from the experience of the Socialist economies. In Hungary, for example, workers began to show an active interest in employee control only after they were given a voice in deciding how the surplus within their own factory should be divided as between the State, reserves and pay packets. In Yugoslavia the workers' incomes depend on financial results of the undertaking and worker decisions as to allocation.

In short, workers can be induced to make greater productive efforts only if they can see that this will have a noticeable effect on their personal earnings—or status or authority. Likewise they will take an active interest in the efficiency of the enterprise—in better organisation and productive methods—only if they can participate through their representatives in making the relevant decisions and protecting themselves against any adverse effects of these decisions. This is why productivity bargaining is proving successful in Britain. And it is also why profit-sharing schemes are likely to spread and to have an effect on productivity only if they are closely associated with machinery for employee participation through which workers can help to decide on how profits are to be shared.

## Productivity Bargaining and Industrial Democracy

Technological and industrial changes are forcing management to become more efficient by making appropriate changes in productive methods and work practices. These changes vitally affect workers and are acceptable to them only with certain major safeguards and guarantees. Workers are learning that the only way they can safeguard their interests is to participate formally in managerial decision-making. Employers are learning that the only way they can secure the assent of workers to change is to allow them so to participate. And productivity bargaining provides a channel through which such participation can take place formally and explicitly at the plant level where the vital changes originate.

Earlier in this chapter a key question was posed: namely, "does the interest of workers in their jobs entitle them to claim the right to co-decision?" The considerations outlined above indicate that the answer is "yes".

This answer implies that the right of co-decision is based upon *power*—the power of workers to interfere with managerial changes which they do not find acceptable. This is a realistic approach. In the words of Clegg:

> Its justification lies in the basic assumption of democracy; that even the most enlightened authorities tend to ignore the interests of others, or to minimise their importance, unless these interests are brought sharply to their attention. Power must be checked by countervailing power.[1]

Or as the TUC puts it:

> Bargaining is a method of reconciling differences of interest to the benefit of both sides. To reconcile different interests does not mean that the interests become the same. It is simply the formal recognition of the common interest of both sides in making a bargain.[2]

In this view, demands for industrial democracy are based not on "common interests" but upon the conflict of interests inherent in the very fabric of industry. Industrial relations are relations between sectional groups with divergent interests. Hence any significant improvements in industrial relations must revolve around new methods of resolving conflicts and of ensuring a fair confrontation

---

[1] Royal Commission on Trade Unions and Employers' Associations, Report No. 1, *loc cit.*

[2] TUC Evidence to Royal Commission on Trade Unions and Employers' Associations, *loc. cit.*, p. 52.

of interests through agreed norms of procedure. Conflict is not incompatible with cooperation, compromise and continuing dialogue.

Conflict is largely over distributive issues. But it is not exclusively or even primarily a struggle between the traditional camps—employers on the one hand and workers on the other. Nor is it limited to distribution of income. Disputes usually relate to conflicts of interest between different groups of employees and they relate to stability as well as level of income, distribution of privileges in terms of job security, job control, job status, authority, working conditions and other fringe benefits. In short, every managerial decision bears within it the seeds of conflict.

Productivity bargaining sharpens the power conflict by bringing divergences of interest into the open and making them explicit. But at the same time it makes it easier to arrive at a fair compromise. It does this by removing the incentives to inefficiency and restrictive work practices, by giving workers a stake in increased productivity and by providing the machinery for continuous participation.

## Summary

The concept of "managerial prerogative", or the right of management to decide unilaterally on vital issues in the workshop, is based upon *ownership* of the business. Increasingly, however, it is being recognised that management must take into account the interests not only of shareholders but also of consumers, of employees and of the general public. The right to manage is closely related to the degree of involvement; decision at each level should be made by those most knowledgeable and most immediately concerned. Although there is a distinct "management function" which is largely a matter of coordination, the exercise of this function is widely diffused. All managers are employees, and all employees exercise some management functions.

Productivity agreements extend the area of formal collective bargaining by removing vital issues from unilateral decision-making by management or by work groups, and bringing them into the framework of joint negotiation and regulation. This reduces the element of arbitrariness in managerial decisions. It also increases the responsibility borne by trade unions at plant level. The principle of devolution of responsibility implies that workers should participate in management through their representatives at every appropriate level. The "appropriate" level is the level at which relevant decisions are taken, and "participation" should take place in discussion units commensurate with the range of effects produced by industrial change.

Productivity bargaining fuses consultation and negotiation into one process of continuous participation, that is, communication, joint determination and continuous adaptation of working practices to technological changes. At certain points, however, the participants agree to disagree, and issues pass out of the stage of joint consultation into that of negotiation, i.e. compromise, through joint collective bargaining machinery. As long as this option is retained, the independence of the unions is not infringed. Productivity bargaining replaces fragmented and informal workplace bargaining with open negotiations between representative bodies at the operative levels at which important issues emerge, and these negotiations result in explicit contractual commitments.

Chapter IX

# Productivity Bargaining and Industrial Change Summary and Conclusions

## Productivity Bargaining has Developed in Response to Industrial Change

Progress in technology, concentration in industry and the continuing shift of productive resources between areas of the country and out of old sectors of industry into new ones—all these changes have had a profound impact on employers, on workers, and hence on the entire system of industrial relations. These developments, in turn, have important implications for economic growth and income distribution.

For *employers,* industrial change has meant an ever-growing scale of production, increased specialisation, and enormous investments in costly machinery and installations with a rapid rate of obsolescence. Productive processes have had to be meshed into highly integrated operations calling for speedier, more accurate and more precise managerial decisions.

A major consequence has been the need for management to become more planning conscious and to seek greater efficiency and control over manpower utilisation in order both to reduce direct labour costs and to achieve more effective use of capital equipment. In recent years, however, this objective has been thwarted by a growing "management gap" compounded of restrictive work practices which have developed as a result of laxity and inertia in management, "cost-plus" mentality, and worker insecurity in the face of technological threats.

These malpractices have been largely the result of industrial change. Demarcation disputes, for instance, are precipitated by the introduction of new methods, new processes, new products and new skill requirements. And overmanning, in turn, is an offshoot of demarcation disputes as well as a form of resistance to the threat of redundancy posed by technological change. Most types of restriction on entry, on upgrading and on output reflect the attempts of craftsmen to stem the erosion through technological development of their professional status and skill differentials, and to retain some measure of control over the relationship between effort and reward. Indeed the growing influence at plant level of work group pressures is evidence enough that management can only cope with the demands of industrial change to the extent that it can obtain the assent and cooperation of its work force.

It is in this context that productivity bargaining can be seen as an extremely useful tool for managerial control. It enables employers to make a frontal attack on restrictive practices in collaboration with workers, not in sterile opposition to them. It facilitates an increase in the interchangeability of the work force; a reduction in number of men required to do the job; elimination of unnecessary overtime and more flexibility in working hours; and overhauling of the wage structure to make it simpler, more stable, more equitable, more of a stimulus to output and more conducive to flexible use of manpower. And in the process of negotiating such changes with workers, management is forced out of its complacency and inertia and obliged to take a critical and coherent look at all the factors which determine labour costs—including particularly the attitudes and requirements of work groups.

For *workers*, the impact of industrial change is even more shattering than it is for employers, because it has a direct and immediate effect on job content, skill and training requirements, level and stability of earnings, promotion prospects, working conditions, individual control over jobs and, not least, employment prospects.

Because of the insecurity engendered by these threats, workers will collaborate in plant adjustments to industrial change only if they are assured of adequate safeguards or compensation against adverse effects of "progress". Otherwise they will resist change.

Hence the significance of productivity bargaining which has been defined as bargaining to make change acceptable. Through open and explicit negotiations at plant or company level workers can, through their trade unions, obtain contractual commitments assuring them of a fair share in the fruits of technological progress and protection against its ill effects. Specifically productivity agreements result in higher earnings, more stable earnings, a more rational and equitable wage structure in the plant or firm, and assurances concerning retraining, promotion, job transfers and redundancy benefits.

## Productivity Bargaining has Far-reaching Implications for Collective Bargaining and Industrial Relations in Britain

In recent years there has been a very marked shift of bargaining from the industry level to the plant level. Actual earnings and hours of work are now largely determined in the workshop rather than in national negotiations.

Many factors have contributed to this extension of the bargaining process to the workshop floor. They include the growing influence of shop stewards, the involvement of works management in grievance procedures, the growth of personnel management and the greater awareness and sophistication of both supervisors and trade union officials in the field of industrial relations techniques.

But the basic reason lies in the fact that any given industry—and particularly the engineering industry which accounts for well over 10 per cent of the total work force—is too diverse within itself to allow of industry-wide standardisation. An industry comprises a large number of firms of different sizes, dealing with a variety of products, utilising many different kinds of technology and equipment and productive methods, and operating in different geographical regions subject to local variations in supply and demand for labour and raw materials. Hence it is not possible at national level to negotiate much more than key minimum rates and general guidelines for differentials, working hours, fringe benefits and shift premia. A great deal has to be left to company and plant bargaining.

It is at the plant level that the effects of changing technology make themselves felt. Technical change can be planned outside the workplace, but it can only be executed *within* it. It is only at the plant level that certain fundamental issues can be tackled. Only at this level is it feasible for the work system to be precisely analysed. It is only at this level that there is real scope for the protracted and comprehensive negotiations which are essential to effective productivity bargaining. It is here that unified management is available capable of participating in the consultations and taking the decisions required. It is at the local level that management can commit itself to specific changes which take account of the distinctive features of the workplace. And finally, it is only at this level that worker participation and involvement can be given real meaning by linking concessions to employees with productivity and labour utilisation.

Thus it has come about that most vital decisions affecting workers are taken at shop level. These include lieu rates, application of job evaluation and of incentive payment schemes, the granting of special payments and bonuses, distribution of work loads, allocation of overtime, promotion, staffing, transfers, discipline, sick benefits, facilities for shop stewards, redundancy, etc. Even more significant, many of the obstacles to efficient use of labour can only be removed by action close to the shop floor. For example, the level of overtime differs greatly between firms and would be expensive to "buy off" right through an industry. Similarly, demarcation rules are often the product of local circumstances or local history, and are not embodied in union rules. There are other issues which are regulated nationally only in terms of minimum conditions or standards but are actually determined locally, for example, piecework prices or terms, other bonus payments and overtime payments, And it is only at plant level that changes in pay can be related to changes in work performance.

Thus most of the benefits obtained by workshop negotiations are not in contravention to national agreements but are supplementary to them. Moreover, it would be difficult to cover them at the national level. In general plant bargains do not conflict with national agreements. Rather they deal with issues that are not covered in national agreements.

This development has been accepted, somewhat reluctantly, by employers—partly because they couldn't do much to prevent it, and partly because they appreciated the flexibility provided by informal and undocumented agreements with shop stewards and work groups which permitted them to compete for workers in a tight labour market by bidding up wages without contractual commitment. At the same time employers have been uneasy about the eroding effect of this development on their managerial prerogatives and on the strength and prestige of employer associations. By the same token they fear that if plant bargaining were to be formalised in a way that weakened the influence of national negotiations, the door would be opened for "whipsawing" tactics by unions and undue pressure on marginal firms.

Similarly, workers and trade unions see both advantages and drawbacks in the trend towards plant bargaining. They appreciate the potential gains in terms of greater efficiency, higher output and increased earnings and also the possibilities for more direct and effective participation by work groups in managerial decision-making. But they are also aware that plant bargaining can, and often does, imply unilateral concessions by employers without intervention of trade unions—especially in view of inadequate trade union organisation at the plant level. This means that workers lose interest in their unions with a consequent serious deterioration in the membership, prestige and bargaining strength of these organisations.

Thus, despite the trend to plant bargaining, national bargaining is still deeply and inextricably woven into the fabric of British industrial relations. Employers are wedded to it, not only out of respect for tradition, but because national standards protect marginal firms and act as a deterrent to "whipsawing" by unions; because national bargaining pools and thereby reinforces the bargaining power of individual employers; and because national negotiations provide a flexible framework within which plant supplements can be suited to local conditions. And trade unions want to retain national bargaining for similar reasons, that is, because it protects marginal workers by facilitating a policy of solidarity; because it prevents competitive wage cutting; because it pools and thereby reinforces the bargaining strength of workers; and because it provides a flexible framework within which work groups can exploit favourable labour markets to obtain increases in earnings above the minimum wage levels negotiated nationally.

Indeed, the importance of industry negotiations in determining earnings, hours and working conditions is actually enhanced by industrial change. This is because, as noted earlier, the impact of industrial change is such that it makes both sides—workers and employers—increasingly conscious of the need to achieve a more rational and fairer wage structure, to avoid inflation and to give trade unions and employers' associations a more important role in shaping national economic policy.

Out of the juxtaposition of these two pressures—the shift to plant bargaining and the continued and increasing stress on industry bargaining for national standards—there has emerged the concept of "two-tier" bargaining. This concept embraces a number of more specific propositions.

In the first place, it implies a fusing of joint consultation and negotiation into a process of "continuous participation" in response to industrial change. This requires the establishment of effective institutional machinery at plant level and, even more important, the development of new attitudes, new channels of communication, new types and sources of information, new organisational structures on both sides and better training and equipping of both management and trade union staff. So far productivity bargaining has acted as a powerful stimulus in each of these respects.

Secondly, two-tier bargaining implies that all important issues affecting earnings, hours and working conditions at plant level should be brought into the collective bargaining framework by being explicitly and formally incorporated into documented contractual agreements between the bargaining parties. Here again productivity bargaining is making a significant contribution. Productivity bargaining is conceived as an exchange of concessions by workers with respect to work practices for concessions by management in terms of sharing the gains resulting from the increased productivity. Hence it is necessary for the elements in the exchange to be identified, measured and specified and then negotiated in considerable detail and the resulting details recorded in a written agreement. Moreover, it is gradually being accepted that broad guidelines for such plant negotiations should be developed for an entire industry at the national level. This in turn considerably strengthens the prestige, authority and responsibility of employer associations and trade unions.

A final implication of two-tier bargaining is the implementation of the notion of industrial democracy or worker participation by giving it real content and significance at the plant level where the most vital issues are decided. In this connection productivity bargaining is playing a crucial role. Productivity agreements remove basic issues from unilateral managerial decision and bring them into the framework of formal collective bargaining for joint determination by both workers and management.

The traditional concept of "managerial prerogative", or the exclusive right of management to decide plant policy, was based on ownership, that is, on the interests of the shareholders. But this approach is being modified through acknowledgement of the other interests affected by managerial decisions—namely, those of consumers, of the wider public, and of the workers whose lives are shaped by their jobs. Accordingly the right to manage is being related to the degree of involvement; and the management function is being recognised as a coordinating function which is exercised in various ways and at various levels by all employees of the firm. The principle of devolution of responsibility delegates decision-making authority to that level at which the relevant decisions have to be taken in response to the issues which make them necessary, and to those individuals most competent to judge the issues.

This development in turn makes clear the necessity of *continuous* consultation and negotiation between management and workers at all levels of the productive process. Productivity bargaining is never finished, because technological change never comes to an end. Thus worker participation must be continuous, and machinery must be provided for this purpose.

In productivity bargaining the processes of consultation and of negotiation remain distinct within a common framework. On some issues and to some extent the two parties can achieve agreement almost without friction; and the more complete the information available and the better the channels of communication, the better are the prospects for effective consultation.

Beyond that point, however, the parties to a productivity agreement must agree to compromise via a process of negotiation. Bargaining implies compromises openly and consciously arrived at. So long as trade unions retain their right to disagree and to negotiate, their independence is intact regardless of the extent of their involvement in managerial decision-making.

### Productivity Bargaining can also Make a Major Contribution to Implementation of a National Incomes Policy

Sustained economic growth in Britain has been inhibited by the persistent problem of rising prices which intermittently leads to deflationary measures resulting in what has come to be known as the "stop-go" economy.

A major factor in this inflationary process has been "wage-drift" or the gap between the rate of actual earnings and of the earnings expected as a result of the wage rates agreed at national level. Wage drift is largely a result of incentive payments and other wage bonuses at the plant level which are very uneven in their impact as between occupations, firms, industry sectors and types of work. This in turn leads to secondary drift through a process of "leapfrogging" in an attempt to correct anomalies and "restore relativities". Thus the inflationary chain reaction of wage–cost–price–wage increases is perpetuated with its serious consequences for individuals, for social stability, for balance of payments equilibrium and for economic growth.

The government has responded to this problem with its prices and incomes policy, and productivity bargaining has been given an important role in that policy. Wage increases up to the 3½ per cent ceiling are authorised where employees make a direct contribution to increased productivity by accepting more exacting work, or major changes in working practices or major reorganisations of wage and salary structures. The only exception to the ceiling on pay increases is that granted to genuine productivity agreements.

Productivity bargaining can help contain earnings drift by bringing about a more rational and equitable wage structure *within* a plant or enterprise. It can do this by consolidating wage rates, cutting down on overtime, tightening up incentive systems, loosening craft demarcations, stimulating occupational mobility, eliminating anomalies within the firm and encouraging joint management-worker decisions.

On the other hand there is no escaping the fact that productivity bargaining may exacerbate "secondary" drift in an industry and the economy as a whole. Because it relates earnings to work practices in a particular plant it necessarily increases differentials between plants—thus adding to inflationary pressures and also offending the basic trade union tenet of "solidarity" or the standard rate for the job.

This is not to say that productivity bargaining is a failure. It must be kept in mind that productivity bargaining was never designed as a way of improving the distribution of income; its purpose is the quite different one of increasing efficiency in the utilisation of manpower. At the same time, however, productivity bargaining cannot evade the issue of "fair shares" because of the important bearing which workers' concern over equity has on their efficiency and their willingness to accept changes in working practices.

## Productivity Bargaining in Perspective

*Experience of productivity bargaining to date clearly warrants the conclusion that it constitutes an invaluable link in a programme for coping with industrial change.*

It appears to be admirably tailored to the particular—and hopefully temporary—situation of the British economy at the present juncture. This is a situation which has been described above in summary fashion as a compound of "management gap" and restrictive work practices.

Certainly productivity bargaining is proving its capacity for changing attitudes on the part of workers and of management, and for sparking off major changes resulting in more efficient utilisation of labour. Also it is stimulating the setting up of machinery for meaningful worker participation in decisions vitally affecting their working lives at plant level. At the same time it is accentuating and focussing the need for negotiation and coordination between representatives of employers and workers at higher levels on certain broader issues thrown into sharp relief by plant bargaining.

On the other hand, it is equally apparent that productivity bargaining is not an *easy* answer to the challenge of industrial change, nor is it the *whole* answer.

*There are several reasons why productivity bargaining is not easy.* The bargaining that precedes the achievement of an agreement is a long, complex, gruelling process of patient negotiation between employers and unions and workers. And the successful implementation of an agreement once it has been accepted is never ending. It involves constant and alert supervision, continuing consultation, and adequate machinery for dealing with grievances which are likely to be more rather than less frequent. It requires management to be more planning conscious, it may involve restructuring of the management hierarchy and particularly strengthening of the personnel department, and it places greatly increased responsibility on supervisory staff. Communications within the plant must be opened up for a full two-way flow of pertinent information. Fundamental improvements are required in the structure, services and training provided to their members by both employer associations and trade unions. Above all, productivity bargaining necessitates basic changes in habits and attitudes of employers and of workers.

*Moreover, productivity bargaining is only one of several solutions which must operate jointly for an effective attack on the problem of industrial change.*

Each of these other links in the chain constitutes a complex issue in itself going far beyond the scope of this book. But for perspective on productivity bargaining it is essential to recognise that its task can only be accomplished in conjunction with these other efforts.

One of these links is the necessity for coordinating the economic planning that takes place at several levels—not only in the plant or company, but also in the industry and on the overall national level. This kind of coordination could be greatly abetted by development of an effective framework for two-tier collective bargaining as described above. It also depends on the kinds of structural improvements in both employers' associations and trade unions that have been stressed in previous pages.

Also there will have to be more effective coordination between trade unions, presumably under the umbrella of the TUC; more effective coordination between employers' associations, presumably under the umbrella of the CBI; and possibly a new organ, not yet blueprinted, for coordination at the national level between the TUC, the CBI and the Government.

An important feature of this kind of coordination is an impartial and independent body, acting on behalf of the community, such as the NBPI, which keeps prices and incomes under constant review. Certainly the shape of the continuing evolution in the work of the Board will have a major bearing on the future success of productivity bargaining in Britain.

Above all, productivity bargaining can prove effective only within a framework which includes an intensive, explicit and coherent attack on the problem of income distribution. Such a programme must include not only a rational and fair wage structure but also greater equity in distributive shares. Thus it involves not only collective bargaining but also the Government's tax, monetary, fiscal and incomes policies which determine the relationships between prices, profits, wages and property incomes.

## The Power Conflict in Industrial Relations

In some ways technological change enhances the power and influence of managers—by reducing worker control over the job, lessening dependence on craft skills and cutting down on the total number of workers required. It also makes it more essential for the management to be in control—because of the need for planning, coordination and precision required by the highly integrated operations that characterise modern production.

By the same token, however, if management is to be able to plan and coordinate, it must be able to rely on the cooperation of its work force. And because technological change poses such serious threats to the security of workers, the problem of obtaining their assent to change has assumed new proportions. In a sense this enhances the potential power of the trade unions. To the extent that they can establish themselves as the champions of the workers in their quest for security they will add new dimensions to their function.

Technological changes have an impact at the company and plant level where production techniques and organisation are decided. Hence it is at this level that productivity bargaining occurs, and it is in productivity bargaining that the new struggle for control is reflected. Until recently employers have been able in general to confine the bargaining process to national negotiations which determined only minimum wages and conditions, allowing them to adapt actual earnings and fringe benefits to their individual circumstances through informal arrangements largely decided unilaterally and not involving them in irreversible commitments.

But productivity bargaining is different. In order to obtain the consent of workers it has become necessary to conclude formal, explicit agreements with trade union officials covering conditions at plant level and leading to establishment of joint machinery for administration of the agreements and continuing discussion and negotiation. Thus employers are finding it necessary to dilute their prerogatives and to share control; and also to expose themselves to the possibility of whipsawing. Small wonder that there have been misgivings and soul-searching on the part of employers' associations.

Trade unions, on the other hand, are faced with serious financial and organisational problems of strengthening their local base and improving channels of communication with, and services to, their plant representatives in order to take advantage of their potential increase in power as a result of productivity bargaining. At the same time they must find a way of reconciling the differentiation inherent in productivity bargaining with their basic tenet of solidarity.

These various problems and issues were not created by productivity bargaining. They were created by industrial change, and they are inherent in any attempt to operate an "incomes policy", and indeed in the operation of centralised collective bargaining at the national level. To some extent productivity bargaining can ease the basic problems by mounting a direct attack on earnings drift. On the other hand, productivity bargaining sharpens the power conflict between management and trade unions, and leaves unresolved certain basic issues as to income distribution within the ranks of wage earners as well as between wage earners and other groups.

Effective economic planning and control of industrial change require participation by the groups concerned at the point where they are affected. Hence there must be continuous day-to-day and year-to-year negotiation and planning working up from the plant level. All interested parties must be brought into the discussion from the outset. They must develop the habit of, and the machinery for, discourse at all levels in order to improve their mutual understanding of requirements for economic efficiency and social justice. "Understanding" is essentially a matter of compromise, but that compromise must be openly and consciously arrived at.

15. Exceptional pay increases should be confined to the following circumstances:

(i) where the employees concerned, for example, by accepting more exacting work or a major change in working practices, make a direct contribution towards increasing productivity in the particular firm or industry. Even in such cases some of the benefit should accrue to the community as a whole in the form of lower prices;

(ii) where it is essential in the national interest to secure a change in the distribution of manpower (or to prevent a change which would otherwise take place) and a pay increase would be both necessary and effective for this purpose;

(iii) where there is general recognition that existing wage and salary levels are too low to maintain a reasonable standard of living;

(iv) where there is widespread recognition that the pay of a certain group of workers has fallen seriously out of line with the level of remuneration for similar work and needs in the national interest to be improved.

Appendix B

# General Guidelines for the Operation of Payment by Results Systems

224. However, the main problem is to determine how far existing PBR systems are working in accordance with the aims of the policy. We think the most useful thing we can do here is to indicate general pointers which can be used to gauge the health of a PBR system. We would emphasise that they are put forward not merely as guides from the standpoint of the policy, but as indicators of good practice to assist managements and workers in the operation of PBR systems. We do not suggest that they should become formal requirements under the incomes policy, although it will obviously be a major concern of the policy to promote the establishment of good payment system practices along these lines.

225. We propose two contrasting sets of guidelines, positive and negative. The first gives indications of success which could be adopted by managers and union negotiators as a standard in seeking to improve their payment systems. The second provides signs of loss of control (a "red light") by which firms may identify their payment systems as urgently needing overhaul. Firms to which this second set of guidelines applies may well need outside aid and should in any case carry out a thorough enquiry into the appropriateness of their present payment system as compared with alternatives.

226. A PBR system is working successfully where:

(*a*) the rate of increase of average hourly earnings (excluding overtime and increases paid under industry-wide agreements or their equivalent in non-federated firms, and excluding also increases demonstratably attributable to increased worker effort) is $1\frac{1}{2}$ per cent or less a year;

(*b*) the proportion of average earnings (excluding overtime) which takes the form of variable output bonus does not exceed one quarter;

(*c*) standards of performance are set by work measurement carried out by adequately trained staff whose consistency in rating is regularly checked;

(*d*) enterprise or industry agreements establish clear ground rules separating the process of pay negotiation from the setting of work standards and ensuring uniformity of practice in respect of the latter;

(*e*) the "learning curve" or "improvement effect" is taken into account when establishing work standards for new jobs and new workers, or revising them for old jobs;

(*f*) the differentials between the pay of different occupational groups are determined in detail by job evaluation, or a systematic and comprehensive agreement (or both), and are specified not merely in terms of basic rates, but of "standard earnings" or the equivalent;

(*g*) the suitability and administration of the system has undergone a major investigation within the past 3 years.

227. We have put forward a figure of 1½ per cent as a measure of acceptable wage drift as defined in guideline (*a*). Although our case studies have shown that some degree of drift appears inevitable even in effectively controlled PBR systems, we think it should be well within the capacity of a properly organised system to keep it below this level.

228. A PBR system is likely to be in urgent need of attention where:

(*a*) the rate of increase of average hourly earnings (excluding overtime and increases paid under industry-wide agreements or their equivalent in non-federated firms, and excluding also increases demonstrably attributable to increased worker effort) exceeds 2½ per cent a year;

(*b*) the proportion of average earnings (excluding overtime) which takes the form of variable output bonus is over one third;

(*c*) the use of work study or measured work standards is not attempted by management, or is prevented or limited by workers;

(*d*) all or most prices and times are fixed by bargaining between individuals or small groups of workers and management representatives, and there is no clear separation of the processes of standard setting and pay negotiation;

(*e*) no account is taken of the "learning curve" or "improvement effect" when establishing work standards for new jobs and new workers, or revising them for old jobs;

(*f*) there are obvious anomalies in the pay of different occupational groups and between workers in different departments;

(*g*) the suitability and administration of the system has not been fully investigated within the past 5 years;

(*h*) where the information necessary to establish (*a*) to (*f*) is lacking.

229. Where a payment system fails to meet the tests of success set out in paragraph 226, without qualifying for urgent attention as indicated in paragraph 228 (e.g. where the amount of average wage drift defined in guideline (*a*) is between $1\frac{1}{2}$ and $2\frac{1}{2}$ per cent) it is possible that control is beginning to slip. Managements should regard this situation as an "amber light" and should be prepared to take remedial action if it worsens further.

230. These guidelines are intended to provide tests of the operation of PBR systems in general and should therefore not be regarded as exhaustive in any particular case. One additional point which may need attention in many industries is the need to ensure that the number of workers, whether direct or indirect, who are paid on "lieu rates" or some equivalent does not represent an undue proportion of the total manual labour force. Managements and union representatives should also consider whether the detailed requirements we specified in Chapter 7 as necessary to ensure the

integrity of a payment system, and adequate joint control of it, are met in their particular case.

231. Enterprises with an effective PBR system should normally have stable or falling unit labour costs; conversely, in those where the system is out of control, labour costs may tend to outstrip productivity. Although these movements should obviously be closely watched, we have avoided incorporating them as specific guidelines, because there is a danger that even when unit labour costs in an enterprise are falling the need for fundamental reforms in the payment system may be obscured. In particular, we have found several cases where there is a high rate of wage drift, but this is still contained within an even higher rate of productivity growth, which is almost entirely due to increased investment or other technical or economic factors in no way associated with the workers' efforts. In such cases of technological change, unit labour costs should be falling even more quickly than they are and the benefits of technical advance, instead of being swallowed up by large increases in wages in the sectors where it occurs, should be passed on to the community in the shape of lower prices.